Contents

Introduction: SnowPro® Core Certifications

Elevate Your Skills Efficiently with QuickTechie's Essential Guide for the Snowflake SnowPro Core Certification

Snowflake, the distinguished cloud-centric data warehousing platform, has garnered significant attention since it emerged in 2014. The platform boasts a range of certification programs, with the SnowPro Core certification standing as a foundational pillar. Achieving the SnowPro Core Certification signifies a profound understanding of Snowflake's role in cloud-based data warehousing, foundational architecture, and the prowess to design, deploy, and manage resilient and scalable Snowflake infrastructures.

https://www.quicktechie.com/ proudly presents its all-encompassing guide, covering every pertinent subject for the Snowflake SnowPro Core Certification examination. Optimize your preparation journey with online mock tests, digital flashcards, a handy e-glossary, and incisive guidance from esteemed domain experts at QuickTechie. With this guide, not only will you be fully equipped to ace the certification, but you'll also possess the hands-on expertise for real-world Snowflake implementations.

Exclusive access to https://www.quicktechie.com/ e-learning hub, replete with chapter-end quizzes, comprehensive mock tests, an array of e-flashcards, and a term glossary.

Perfect for aspirants eyeing a future in cloud-data warehousing or seasoned database aficionados keen on familiarizing with the latest in data solutions, QuickTechie's Snowflake SnowPro Core Certification Guide is a must-have resource.

This book is tailored by https://www.quicktechie.com/ to set you on the path to success for the SnowPro Core Certification exam. With the expertise of seasoned professionals at www.QuickTechie.com, this resource ensures that you won't have to navigate your preparation journey alone. The chapters in this manual mirror the exam domains outlined on Snowflake's official site. By delving into this material, you're setting yourself up with a profound understanding, amplifying your chances of acing the exam and securing the esteemed certification.

Each question of this book offers clear explanations, step-by-step instructions, practical advice, and invaluable insights tailored to the exam's specifics. www.QuickTechie.com ensures that you stay on track by focusing on what truly matters for the exam, eliminating any unnecessary complexities or overly advanced content that might divert your attention.

Exam Overview: SnowPro® Core Certifications

As you embark on your journey to prepare for the SnowPro Core Certification with "www.QuickTechie.com," you're taking a pivotal step towards mastering the intricacies of the Snowflake Data Cloud.

This section of the "www.QuickTechie.com" certification preparation guide serves as your compass, guiding you through the essentials you need to be exam-ready. Dive deep into the tools and resources that will shape your study approach. Understand the process of acquiring a demo Snowflake account, granting you a hands-on experience to reinforce your theoretical knowledge. Our book, with its repository of 200 meticulously crafted questions, will test your grasp on the subject. Additionally, the guide offers valuable links to further reading materials and provides a step-by-step procedure on how to enroll for the examination.

Exam Content Overview from www.QuickTechie.com

Introducing the SnowPro Core Certification Preparation Book, tailored for aspirants eager to demonstrate their proficiency in Snowflake. This comprehensive guide by www.QuickTechie.com aids you in mastering the following domains, with 200 expertly crafted questions to ensure you are well-prepared:

1. Techniques for data loading and its transformation within Snowflake
2. Insights into virtual warehouse efficacy and concurrent operations

3. Crafting DDL and DML commands efficiently
4. Practical approaches to handle semi-structured and unstructured datasets
5. Grasping the concepts of cloning and time-travel functionalities
6. Deep dive into data distribution methods
7. Structuring and efficiently managing your Snowflake account

While the core of this preparation material won't delve into the essentials of cloud foundations or basic SQL syntax, it is assumed that learners possess a grounding in these areas. Here are some foundational pillars that candidates should ideally be conversant with:

- Fundamentals of databases, inclusive of standard terminologies and core SQL operations like data selection and manipulation.
- An introductory understanding of database components, spanning from tables and views to more advanced elements like stored procedures and functions.
- Vital security paradigms, accentuating the nuances differentiating authentication from authorization.
- A panoramic view of cloud infrastructure, its services, and architectural frameworks.

Dive deep into Snowflake with confidence, armed with the preparation resources from www.QuickTechie.com. Ensure you are exam-ready!

Certification Preparation Overview by www.QuickTechie.com

When preparing for your certification with www.QuickTechie.com, it's essential to understand the primary subject areas of focus, as highlighted in Table 1-1 below.

Table 1-1: Key Subject Domains and Their Relative Importance

Table 1-1 showcases the estimated weighting for each domain area. This is a representation of how frequently each topic will appear in the 200 questions of our certification book.

Domain Areas	Proportion of Weightage
Features and Architecture of the Snowflake Cloud Data Platform	20 – 25%
Secure Access and Account Safety	20 – 25%
Principles of Performance	10 – 15%
Techniques for Data Input and Output	5 – 10%
Procedures for Data Transformations	20 – 25%
Methods for Data Safety and Sharing	5 – 10%

As per guidelines provided by www.QuickTechie.com, while the table captures major domains, it doesn't encompass every detail that might come up in the exam. Thus, as an aspirant, it's recommended to dive deep into all the subjects in the study guide provided, as well as additional resources and topics covered in the www.QuickTechie.com certification preparation book.

Exam Structure

www.QuickTechie.com presents its certification examination that has been structured meticulously to evaluate your proficiency. The examination booklet contains a total of 200 preparation questions, of which 100 will appear on the actual test. Here's a breakdown of the question types you can anticipate:

Single Choice Questions: Choose the most suitable option from the given choices.

Multiple Response Questions: Depending on the directive provided, pick all relevant responses.

The duration specified for the examination is 115 minutes. If you've effectively utilized the resources and questions from www.QuickTechie.com's guide, you should find it feasible to answer all queries within the provided timeframe. It's worth noting that certain questions are inserted for statistical analysis and won't influence your overall score. Such questions are indistinguishable and aren't marked.

To succeed in this examination, you need to achieve a score of 750, with the total possible score being 1000. For any updates or additional details about this certification examination, we recommend visiting the Certification Section on www.QuickTechie.com.

Exam Procedures and Resit Guidelines by www.QuickTechie.com

When taking the certification exam from www.QuickTechie.com, ensure you are present at the designated location and time. After finishing the test, www.QuickTechie.com will send an email detailing your performance on the exam.

Successfully passing the test will be marked as 'Pass' on your transcript, and your specific score will be disclosed. If you clear the exam, expect an email from Credly within the next 72 hours. It's essential to claim your digital badge and formalize your certification from www.QuickTechie.com.

In cases where you don't secure a passing grade, your transcript will reflect 'Fail', and you'll be provided with a detailed score and feedback. But don't get disheartened! Delve back into the study resources available on www.QuickTechie.com, pay special attention to the areas of improvement highlighted in your feedback, and consider resitting the test.

For those attempting the SnowPro Core Certification, remember that after an unsuccessful attempt, you must wait seven days before trying again. Within a year, you have the opportunity to attempt this exam up to four times. It's crucial to note that every attempt is charged, and www.QuickTechie.com doesn't offer complimentary resits or discounts for subsequent tries.

Recertification Details by www.QuickTechie.com

Snowflake's ever-evolving nature means it's essential to ensure your certification remains relevant. All Snowflake certifications have a two-year validity. To maintain your qualification, you can enroll for the concise SnowPro Core Recertification Exam offered by www.QuickTechie.com and secure a passing grade, thus renewing your SnowPro Core Certification for another two years.

Alternatively, consider enrolling for the SnowPro Advanced Certification through www.QuickTechie.com. Clearing this exam will automatically update the validity of your SnowPro Core Certification in line with the new Advanced Certification's expiry.

Summary

This segment has outlined all vital aspects to gear you up for the SnowPro Core Certification exam through www.QuickTechie.com. It has given insights into the exam's structure, question types, and even guided you on availing a 30-day complimentary trial Snowflake account. Using this trial, you can gain practical exposure to Snowflake and hone your skills with hands-on tasks present in this guide.

Stay tuned for the upcoming chapter from www.QuickTechie.com, where we will introduce you to the dynamic world of the Snowflake Cloud Data platform, marking the next step in your learning journey with Snowflake.

About Snowflake Cloud Data

Snowflake emerges as the pioneer in analytic database technology, explicitly conceived and constructed for the cloud environment. Offered as a Software-as-a-Service (SaaS), Snowflake showcases enhanced performance, user-friendliness, and versatility when juxtaposed with conventional databases.

This section delves into the foundational attributes of the Snowflake Cloud Data ecosystem. It casts light on the diverse Snowflake versions available, the cloud infrastructures it aligns with, and the global regions it can operate within. Additionally, the chapter underscores the multifaceted avenues through which one can engage with Snowflake - be it through its web-based user interface, the command-line terminal, or via various connectors.

To ensure readers can seamlessly transition to hands-on exercises detailed in the following sections, this chapter further guides through a concise preliminary configuration of your Snowflake account.

Snowflake: A Comprehensive Cloud Service

Snowflake offers a holistic cloud service encompassing data storage, processing (including data load and unload operations), and analytic solutions accessible through SQL or compatible programming languages. It mirrors the features of conventional databases, encompassing user authentication, authorization, data security, high uptime, and performance fine-tuning. Snowflake has a few unique cloud-centric traits:

-   It thrives entirely on cloud platforms, barring a few exceptions like optional command-line tools, drivers, and connectors. There's zero hardware overhead.

- Snowflake oversees all software installations and updates, eliminating the need for users to engage in manual configurations or setups.
- Regular maintenance and system upgrades? Snowflake has it covered. Users enjoy a hassle-free experience.

Cloud Platforms Supporting Snowflake

Being a cloud-native service, Snowflake integrates seamlessly with leading cloud providers. Users can establish their Snowflake account on any of the ensuing platforms:

- Amazon Web Services (AWS)
- Microsoft Azure (Azure)
- Google Cloud Platform (GCP)

The choice of the cloud platform is made when initiating a Snowflake account. Each platform offers multiple regions for account provisioning, ensuring a global reach and flexibility.

Snowflake Edition Options

Snowflake presents a range of editions tailored to cater to different organizational requirements. Every upgraded edition not only encompasses the features of its predecessor but also introduces additional functionalities or enhanced service levels. Organizations have the flexibility to modify their chosen Snowflake edition within their existing account as per evolving needs.

The selected Snowflake edition plays a pivotal role in defining the pricing for consumed credits and data storage. Other pricing determinants include the regional location of the Snowflake account and its category, which could be:

- **On-demand Account:** This offers a flexible pricing model based on actual usage without the need for long-term licensing agreements.
- **Capacity Account**: Here, prices are reduced in exchange for a pre-determined capacity commitment.

Let's delve deeper into each Snowflake edition:

Standard Edition

At its core, the Standard edition encompasses all foundational features offered by Snowflake, without any restrictions. Organizations aiming for an optimal mix of features, support, and affordability will find this edition apt.

Enterprise Edition

Building on the Standard edition's capabilities, the Enterprise edition introduces several advanced functionalities designed for larger enterprises. Notable features include 90-day time travel, routine re-encryption of data, granular security at column and row levels, object tagging and categorization, the advantage of multi-cluster virtual warehouses, enhanced search capabilities, materialized view options, and a comprehensive record of user access.

Business Critical Edition

The Business Critical edition, while integrating all the offerings of the Enterprise edition, ups the ante in data protection. This edition is tailor-made for organizations handling extremely sensitive data, such as personal health records, necessitating stringent compliance with industry standards. Distinctive features comprise user-controlled encryption keys, exclusive cloud provider connectivity, and seamless database transition between Snowflake accounts, ensuring uninterrupted business operations and robust disaster recovery protocols.

Virtual Private Snowflake (VPS)

The pinnacle of Snowflake editions, the VPS, not only encompasses the offerings of the Business Critical edition but goes a step further in security provisions. Accounts under this edition benefit from a secluded environment, distinctly separated from other Snowflake accounts, ensuring maximum data security. Such rigorous security measures make the VPS edition the top choice for entities like financial institutions with paramount data protection needs.

FAQ: SnowPro® Core Certifications

Question-1: What is the purpose of the SnowPro® Core Certification?

Answer: The SnowPro® Core Certification is designed for individuals who want to demonstrate their knowledge of the Snowflake Data Cloud.

Question-2: What areas of knowledge does the SnowPro® Core Certification cover?

Answer: The candidate will be tested on:

- Data Loading and Transformation in Snowflake
- Virtual Warehouse Performance and Concurrency
- DDL and DML Queries
- Using Semi-Structured and Unstructured Data
- Cloning and Time Travel
- Data Sharing
- Snowflake Account Structure and Management

Question-3: What experience is recommended for a SnowPro® Core Certification candidate?

Answer: It is recommended for the candidate to have at least 6 months of practical experience with Snowflake.

Question-4: How many questions are in the exam?

Answer: There are a total of 100 questions in the exam.

Question-5: What types of questions are included in the exam?

Answer: The exam contains Multiple Select and Multiple Choice questions.

Question-6: How much time is given to complete the exam?

Answer: Candidates have 115 minutes to complete the exam.

Question-7: In which languages is the exam available?

Answer: The exam is available in both English and Japanese.

Question-8: How much does the registration for the exam cost?

Answer: The registration fee for the exam is $175 USD.

**Question-9: What is the passing score for the SnowPro®
Core Certification exam?**

Answer: The passing score is 750+, with a scaled scoring
system from 0 - 1000.

Question-10: Are there any unscored content in the exam?

Answer: Yes, exams may include unscored items to gather
statistical information for future use. These items are not
identified on the form, don't affect the score, and additional
time is factored for this content.

**Question-11: Are there any prerequisites for taking the
exam?**

Answer: No, there are no prerequisites for the exam.

Question-12: What are the delivery options for the exam?

Answer: The exam can be taken through Online Proctoring or
at Onsite Testing Centers.

**Question-13: Does the exam guide offer a comprehensive
list of all content on the examination?**

Answer: No, the exam guide includes test domains,
weightings, and objectives but is not a comprehensive listing
of all content that will be presented.

**Question-14: Can you detail the content domains and their
weightings for the exam?**

Answer: Certainly. The main content domains and their weightings are:

- Snowflake Data Cloud Features & Architecture: 25%
- 2.0 Account Access and Security: 20%
- 3.0 Performance Concepts: 15%
- 4.0 Data Loading and Unloading: 10%
- 5.0 Data Transformations: 20%
- 6.0 Data Protection and Data Sharing: 10%

Question-15: What is the exam version for SnowPro® Core Certification?

Answer: The exam version is COF-C02.

Question-16: If I don't pass the SnowPro® Core Certification exam on my first try, is there a waiting period to retake it?

Answer: The provided information doesn't specify a waiting period, but it's common for certification exams to have a waiting period or increased fee for retakes. It's best to check with the official Snowflake website or contact the exam provider for details.

Question-17: Are there any resources or courses recommended to prepare for the exam?

Answer: While the provided information doesn't mention specific resources, candidates typically benefit from official Snowflake training, documentation, hands-on experience, and preparation materials available on Quicktechie.com.

Question-18: How is the exam proctored during online testing?

Answer: The online proctoring option means that candidates are monitored via their computer's webcam and microphone throughout the duration of the exam to ensure the integrity of the exam environment. Specific rules and setup details would be provided upon choosing this option.

Question-19: Can I use reference materials during the exam?

Answer: The provided details don't specify, but typically, certification exams are closed book. It's essential to check the guidelines provided upon registration or consult the official Snowflake website.

Question-20: Do the unscored items in the exam consume part of the allocated 115 minutes?

Answer: Yes, while the unscored items do not impact your final score, the time taken to answer them is part of the overall 115 minutes. Additional time has been factored into the total to account for these questions.

Question-21: Can I take the exam in any language other than English and Japanese?

Answer: As per the provided information, the exam is currently available only in English and Japanese.

Question-22: Are there any accommodations for individuals with disabilities?

Answer: The provided information does not specify, but certification exam providers typically offer accommodations for candidates with disabilities. It would be best to contact the exam provider directly for specific accommodations.

Question-23: How soon after the exam will I receive my results?

Answer: The information provided does not specify the result turnaround time, but many certification exams offer immediate preliminary results upon completion. It's recommended to check with the exam provider for specifics.

Question-24: Is there an expiration date for the SnowPro® Core Certification once obtained?

Answer: The provided information doesn't mention an expiration date, but certifications often need renewal or continuing education. Check the official Snowflake website or certification guidelines for details.

SnowPro Practice Paper-1

Question-1: Envision a scenario in which your task is to monitor and manage the records present in external tables. In this context, which stream type do you think will best serve your needs?

A. A stream type with an exclusive append data feature.

B. A stream type that has been exclusively crafted for managing external tables.

C. A stream type with functionality solely to insert data.

D. A conventional or standard stream type.

Correct Answer: C

Explanation: In the realm of Snowflake, when you want to keep tabs on the records of external tables, the "Insert-only" stream emerges as the most suitable. This stream type is distinct from others, primarily because it lets you monitor any fresh data that's inserted post the stream's creation.

Question-2: Suppose you want to ensure that floating-point numbers retain their accuracy without truncation upon data unloading. In this situation, which file format will you opt for?

A. A file format like Comma-Separated Values (CSV).

B. A format resembling JavaScript Object Notation (JSON).

C. An Optimized Row Columnar (ORC) file configuration.

D. A Parquet styled file.

Correct Answer: D

Explanation: The Parquet file format is a columnar storage setup, tailor-made to be compatible with big data processing systems. One of its major advantages is its ability to keep floating-point numbers precise during data unloading, thereby avoiding any accidental truncation.

Question-3: Let's say you possess semi-structured data that you wish to load into Snowflake, yet you're uncertain about the possible operations you might execute on it. Given this uncertainty, which column type does Snowflake endorse?

A. A column type fashioned as ARRAY.

B. An OBJECT-styled column type.

C. A column with a TEXT type.

D. A VARIANT oriented column type.

Correct Answer: D

Explanation: For datasets that are semi-structured in nature, Snowflake highly recommends the VARIANT column type. This type is versatile, self-explanatory, and capable of accommodating values from varied types, encompassing intricate objects and arrays. It's ideally compatible with formats like JSON, Avro, ORC, and Parquet.

Question-4: Of the Snowflake entities mentioned below, which one stands out as a crucial tool for gauging the efficiency of a virtual warehouse, especially when affected by query queuing?

A. The object termed as Resource Monitor.

B. The entity named Account_usage.query_history.

C. The object under Information_schema.warehouse_load_history.

D. The Information_schema.warehouse_metering_history entity.

Correct Answer: B

Explanation: For a comprehensive analysis of a virtual warehouse's efficiency, especially when impeded by query queuing, the Account_usage.query_history object proves invaluable. This object furnishes in-depth insights into Snowflake's query activities, paving the way for enhanced performance assessment and optimization.

Question-5: Among the listed Snowflake entities, can you identify the one that boasts the unique feature of temporary creation?

A. The entity referred to as the Role object.

B. The entity termed as the Stage object.

C. The User-centric object.

D. The object known as Storage Integration.

Correct Answer: B

Explanation: Within Snowflake's architecture, it's the Stage object that has the capability of temporary instantiation. Stage objects are special; they serve as interim holding zones for data files before these files find their way into the Snowflake database. Depending on the use case, these can be either temporary or enduring.

Question-6: When it comes to efficient data management within Snowflake, what's the recommended approach to transport data to a cloud storage destination?

A. Leveraging an external tool to streamline the data unloading trajectory towards cloud storage.

B. Undertaking a direct unloading operation to relay the data to the designated cloud storage area.

C. Starting by unloading data onto a local system, subsequently uploading it to the cloud storage.

D. Initially unloading the data onto a user stage, then advancing to upload it to the cloud storage.

Correct Answer: B

Explanation: The pinnacle of efficiency in offloading data from Snowflake to a specific cloud storage location is achieved by doing it directly. This method bypasses the need for supplementary transfer phases or external tool engagement, leading to a more cohesive and economically sound data management paradigm.

Question-7: Which command is earmarked to retrieve files from both internal and external stages and save them to a local system?

A. The command known as COPY INTO.

B. The command labeled GET.

C. The PUT command.

D. The command titled TRANSFER.

Correct Answer: B

Explanation: In Snowflake's command repertoire, the GET command stands out for its role in unloading files. When called upon, it procures data files from stages (be it internal or external), unloads them effectively, and safely houses them in a local storage environment.

Question-8: When conceptualizing a tabular User-Defined Function (UDF) in SQL, which keyword finds its place within the return clause?

A. The keyword ROW_NUMBER.

B. The keyword TABLE.

C. The keyword TABULAR.

D. The keyword VALUES.

Correct Answer: B

Explanation: For tabular User-Defined Functions (UDF) in SQL, the "TABLE" keyword is paramount. It signifies the function's capacity to return a table, a feature that can be harnessed in ensuing queries.

Question-9: Among the provided SQL statements, can you pinpoint the one that mandates an active virtual warehouse for its execution?

A. Running the command SELECT COUNT(*) FROM TBL_EMPLOYEE;

B. Applying the command ALTER TABLE TBL_EMPLOYEE ADD COLUMN EMP_REGION VARCHAR(20);

C. Executing the command INSERT INTO TBL_EMPLOYEE(EMP_ID, EMP_NAME, EMP_SALARY, DEPT) VALUES(1, 'Adam', 20000, 'Finance');

D. Initiating the command CREATE OR REPLACE TABLE TBL_EMPLOYEE (EMP_ID NUMBER, EMP_NAME VARCHAR(30), EMP_SALARY NUMBER, DEPT VARCHAR(20));

Correct Answer: C

Explanation: The SQL directive "INSERT INTO TBL_EMPLOYEE(EMP_ID, EMP_NAME, EMP_SALARY, DEPT) VALUES(1, 'Adam', 20000, 'Finance');" unequivocally demands a live virtual warehouse. Snowflake emphasizes that Data Manipulation Language (DML) actions, like INSERT, require an operational warehouse for successful statement execution.

Question-10: In the context of REST APIs, which of the listed endpoints is optimally suited for managing unstructured data?

A. The API endpoint insertFiles.

B. The API endpoint insertReport.

C. The API endpoint GET /api/files/.

D. The API endpoint loadHistoryScan.

Correct Answer: C

Explanation: The REST API pathway "GET /api/files/" is intuitively designed for unstructured data interactions. It offers unobstructed access to files or directory structures, empowering users to navigate and collaborate with unstructured data efficiently.

Question-11: Which of these given choices accurately presents a SQL query that incorporates a URL of a file, hosted by Snowflake, located within a directory table of a stage named 'bronzestage'?

A. Implementing the command list @bronzestage;

B. Executing the command select * from directory(@bronzestage);

C. Initiating the command select metadata$filename from @bronzestage;

D. Executing the query select * from table(information_schema.stage_directory_file_registration_ history(stage_name=>'bronzestage'));

Correct Answer: B

Explanation: In Snowflake, the appropriate method to list all files in a specified directory of a stage, such as 'bronzestage', and thereby include Snowflake-hosted file URLs is by using the "select * from directory(@bronzestage);" command.

Question-12: Which specific tool or feature is seamlessly integrated into Snowflake's ecosystem to provide robust support for Multi-Factor Authentication (MFA)?

A. Authy

B. Duo Security

C. One Login

D. RSA SecurID Access

Correct Answer: B

Explanation: For enhanced security, Snowflake has incorporated support for Multi-Factor Authentication (MFA) by partnering with Duo Security. This ensures an additional layer of defense against unauthorized access to user accounts.

Question-13: Within Snowflake's architectural design, which specific layer takes charge of restructuring data into a highly optimized, compacted, and columnar format?

A. Cloud Services

B. Database Storage

C. Query Processing

D. Metadata Management

Correct Answer: B

Explanation: The Database Storage layer in Snowflake's architecture plays a pivotal role where it autonomously manages data. This layer ensures data is compressed, encrypted, and structured in a format optimized for columnar storage.

Question-14: Under which exact condition are session variables, defined by users, made available for access within a scripted procedure in Snowflake?

A. When explicitly declared using the STRICT parameter.

B. If the procedure is designed with the intention to execute in the CALLER's context.

C. When the mode of procedure execution is set as OWNER.

D. Whenever the procedure is described with an argument that matches the session variable in both name and data type.

Correct Answer: B

Explanation: For scripting in Snowflake, the accessibility of session variables is ensured when the procedure is designed to execute within the CALLER's context. This mechanism facilitates the sharing and manipulation of these variables throughout various segments of the procedure.

Question-15: When engineers endeavor to craft User-Defined Functions (UDFs) by leveraging the capabilities of the Snowpark API, which programming language are they presented with as an option?

A. Swift

B. JavaScript

C. Python

D. SQL

Correct Answer: C

Explanation: As per information available up to September 2021, the Snowpark API empowers developers to design User-Defined Functions (UDFs) specifically using the Python programming language. However, it is always prudent to consult the latest Snowflake documentation for any updates.

Question-16: Imagine a scenario where a user has a data size of 1 GB, located in an external stage. The user intends to incorporate this data using the COPY INTO command. What would be the most efficient strategy to undertake this operation ensuring peak performance and minimal expenditure?

A. Process the data as a unified, compressed file.

B. Ingest the data as one uncompressed file.

C. Segment the data into multiple smaller files, each ranging between 100-250 MB, compress them, and then ingest these files.

D. Split the data into fragments of 100-250 MB each and then ingest these uncompressed segments.

Correct Answer: C

Explanation: For optimized ingestion in Snowflake, data should ideally be broken down into more manageable chunks, preferably compressed, in the 100-250MB range. This strategy leverages parallel processing, resulting in enhanced performance while keeping costs low.

Question-17: Given a user operating in Snowflake has two tables with numerical values. To determine the values that overlap in both tables, which SQL set operator is most apt?

A. INTERSECT

B. MERGE

C. MINUS

D. UNION

Correct Answer: A

Explanation: The SQL set operator "INTERSECT" is tailored to identify overlapping values between two datasets. When executed, it provides the intersection of rows yielded by both the SELECT statements involved.

Question-18: Envision a situation where a permanent table serves as a base for a defined view. Subsequently, a temporary table, sharing the same name as the permanent table, is instantiated in the identical schema. In this configuration, what outcome can one anticipate when querying the view?

A. Retrieves data from the original permanent table.

B. Accesses data from the newly created temporary table.

C. Returns an error message, indicating an inability to compile the view.

D. Flags an error stating that the referenced object's identity is ambiguous.

Correct Answer: B

Explanation: Snowflake's architecture prioritizes temporary tables over permanent ones when they share the same name and exist in the same schema. Therefore, any query targeting that table name will fetch data from the temporary table.

Question-19: In Snowflake's suite of file functions, which specific function is purpose-built to generate a URL (hosted by Snowflake) for a staged file by accepting the name of the stage and the relative file path?

A. BUILD_STAGE_FILE_URL

B. GET_ABSOLUTE_PATH

C. GET_RELATIVE_PATH

D. GET_STAGE_LOCATION

Correct Answer: A

Explanation: In the Snowflake environment, the function "BUILD_STAGE_FILE_URL" is meticulously designed to produce a Snowflake-hosted URL that corresponds to a staged file. It achieves this by requiring two primary inputs: the name of the stage and the file's relative path.

Question-20: Snowflake offers a myriad of services and features. Among these, which one is specially crafted to bolster the efficiency of distinct lookup and analytical queries, especially those that heavily rely on a vast array of WHERE clauses?

A. Data classification

B. Query acceleration service

C. Search optimization service

D. Tagging

Correct Answer: C

Explanation: Snowflake's "Search Optimization Service" stands out as a distinctive feature. It is tailored to amplify the performance of certain query types. This service is particularly potent for queries laden with extensive WHERE conditions, as it provides a streamlined methodology for data retrieval.

Question-21: When using SnowSQL, which specific file is responsible for holding crucial connection-related data, such as user credentials and account details?

A. Is it the "history" file?

B. Could it be the "config" file?

C. Maybe it's the "snowsql.cnf" file?

D. Or is it the "snowsql.pubkey" file?

Correct Answer: B

Explanation: In SnowSQL, the file named "config" is pivotal for storing essential connection parameters. This configuration file archives a variety of information, including user credentials, account specifics, and other related details.

Question-22: In Snowflake, how does the performance of secure views compare to their non-secure counterparts?

A. Do secure views operate more slowly than non-secure ones?

B. In data sharing situations, do non-secure views receive precedence?

C. Are secure views highly performant, similar to materialized views?

D. Is there a negligible performance gap between the two?

Correct Answer: A

Explanation: Within Snowflake, secure views tend to operate at a slower pace in comparison to non-secure views. This is primarily because they incorporate an extra layer for data security, ensuring indirect data exposure is minimized, which inherently demands more computational power.

Question-23: When implementing a SQL join, which specific type ensures that every row from a designated table is enumerated, even if no corresponding match exists in another table?

A. Could it be a cross join?

B. Perhaps an inner join?

C. A natural join, maybe?

D. Or is it an outer join?

Correct Answer: D

Explanation: In SQL, an outer join is distinct in that it displays all rows from a given table, including those lacking a counterpart in another table. It synergizes the effects of both left and right joins.

Question-24: When transferring data to an external storage stage in Snowflake, what is the utmost file size that it can accommodate?

A. Can it handle up to 1 GB?

B. Or does it support up to 5 GB?

C. Perhaps it's 10 GB?

D. Or even as large as 16 GB?

Correct Answer: B

Explanation: When you're offloading data to an external stage within Snowflake, the system can manage files that are up to 5 GB in size. Such a limitation ensures that data handling and transfers remain efficient.

Question-25: Over what period does Snowflake's ACCESS_HISTORY view store and maintain access-related data?

A. For a brief span of 7 days?

B. A more extended period of 14 days?

C. Does it cover an entire month, i.e., 28 days?

D. Or an extensive duration of 365 days?

Correct Answer: D

Explanation: Snowflake's ACCESS_HISTORY view is designed to preserve data access details for a comprehensive period of 365 days. It acts as a meticulous record, aiding in the monitoring of Snowflake account activity over the past year.

Question-26: To activate client-side encryption for a directory table within Snowflake, which encryption type is utilized?

A. Is it AES?

B. Could it be AWS_CSE?

C. Maybe SNOWFLAKE_SSE?

D. Or is it the SNOWFLAKE_FULL method?

Correct Answer: D

Explanation: In Snowflake, to guarantee client-side encryption for a directory table, the "SNOWFLAKE_FULL" encryption method is employed. It reinforces optimal data security by encrypting content both at rest and during transit.

Question-27: Suppose file format settings are given in various places. In such a scenario, which setting holds the primary precedence during a data load operation?

A. Is it the table's specific definition?

B. Or the definition of the stage?

C. Could it be at the session level?

D. Or primarily within the COPY INTO TABLE command?

Correct Answer: D

Explanation: If file format parameters are declared in multiple areas, the COPY INTO TABLE directive is prioritized during data loading operations. Owing to its high precedence, this command can supersede other settings.

Question-28: If a multifaceted SQL query, involving several tables and joins, exhibits prolonged execution times, and after inspecting the Query Profile, it's evident that every partition is scanned, what's the probable culprit for this performance issue?

A. Could it be a flawed execution of pruning mechanisms?

B. Is it the sheer data retrieval volume, compounded by multiple joins?

C. Perhaps it's the use of inappropriate joins, which trigger broad scans and fetch superfluous records?

D. Or might it necessitate a refined ordering for the columns within the micro-partitions based on specific dataset attributes?

Correct Answer: A

Explanation: In circumstances where all partitions undergo scanning, it's indicative of a compromised pruning operation. Efficient pruning in Snowflake is instrumental in sidestepping unnecessary micro-partitions, thereby enhancing query performance.

Question-29: What is the primary kind of support that Snowflake's search optimization service provides?

A. Does it cater to external tables?

B. Perhaps it's tailored for materialized views?

C. Is it specialized for tables and views that remain unprotected by specific row access policies?

D. Or does it extend to casting on table columns, with an exception for fixed-point numbers cast to textual representations?

Correct Answer: C

Explanation: The primary focus of Snowflake's search optimization service lies in offering support for tables and views that aren't shielded by row access regulations. By doing so, it significantly elevates the efficacy and speed of database searches within Snowflake.

Question-30: In Snowflake, which category of table becomes inaccessible post the termination of a session, thereby being devoid of both Fail-safe and Time Travel recovery mechanisms?

A. Are these the external tables?

B. Maybe they are the permanent ones?

C. Or are they temporary tables?

D. Could it be the transient tables?

Correct Answer: C

Explanation: Snowflake's temporary tables have a unique trait: they are bound to the session in which they were created. Once that specific session concludes, these tables cease to exist. Consequently, they don't possess Fail-safe or Time Travel recovery features.

Question-31: When considering how many network policies can be simultaneously assigned to a particular account or an individual user within Snowflake, what is the maximum limit?

A. Only one network policy.

B. A maximum of two.

C. Up to three.

D. There's no specific limit, it's unlimited.

Correct Answer: A

Explanation: Within the Snowflake environment, there's a restriction which allows just one network policy to be linked with either an account or a specific user at any given point. The rationale behind this is to establish and enforce stringent access control measures, ensuring there's no room for discrepancies.

Question-32: When we think about a tag in connection with a data masking policy, which statement accurately describes its characteristics?

A. Once a masking policy is attached, it's possible to remove the associated tag.

B. For each distinct data type, a tag is allowed to have just one masking policy.

C. For every type of data, a tag might have several masking policies.

D. Depending on varying data types, a tag can possess different masking policies.

Correct Answer: B

Explanation: Focusing on data masking policies, it's essential to note that a tag is designed to have a single masking policy for every specific data type. Such a design choice ensures that things remain transparent and minimizes the potential for any overlapping or conflicting masking policies.

Question-33: For which client interfaces or tools does Snowflake extend its support for Multi-Factor Authentication (MFA) token caching? Select the two correct options.

A. The GO driver interface.

B. The Node.js driver tool.

C. The ODBC driver platform.

D. The connector designed for Python.

E. The connector tailored for Spark.

Correct Answer: C, D

Explanation: The Snowflake platform has enhanced its security framework by offering MFA token caching capabilities specifically for the ODBC driver and the connector used for Python. This advanced security measure provides an augmented level of authentication, particularly for these client Interfaces.

Question-34: When looking at the Activity section in Snowsight, which pages can one expect to find? Choose the two appropriate options.

A. Contacts page.

B. Settings related to sharing.

C. The history of copying operations.

D. A comprehensive history of executed queries.

E. The history of automatic clustering processes.

Correct Answer: C, D

Explanation: The Snowsight's Activity segment prominently features the 'Copy History' and 'Query History' pages. Such pages are instrumental in offering detailed insights regarding previous actions, enabling users to dive deep into troubleshooting and comprehensively analyze performance metrics.

Question-35: Within the Snowsight's Activity section, what crucial action can a Snowflake user undertake?

A. They can craft visually appealing dashboards.

B. They have the capability to author and execute SQL-based queries.

C. It allows them to delve into databases and explore various objects.

D. They can meticulously analyze the efficiency of queries that have been run.

Correct Answer: D

Explanation: In Snowsight's Activity section, users are given a platform where they can deeply analyze the efficacy of queries that have been previously executed. This in-built utility aids users in monitoring query activities, diagnosing potential issues, and optimizing the performance of the entire query execution process.

Question-36: At which crucial juncture is the data subjected to encryption when leveraging the PUT command within Snowflake?

A. Once it is directed towards the virtual warehouse.

B. During the micro-partitioning phase.

C. Prior to its transmission from the user's computing device.

D. Post its arrival at the designated internal staging area.

Correct Answer: C

Explanation: Utilizing the PUT command in Snowflake ensures that data undergoes encryption before initiating the transmission from the user's machine. Such a security measure is of paramount importance as it guarantees the safety and confidentiality of data throughout its transit.

Question-37: Which column varieties are endorsed by Snowflake for effective use as clustering keys? Opt for the two most relevant columns.

A. The VARIANT column type.

B. Columns that exhibit extremely low cardinality.

C. Columns that showcase extremely high cardinality.

D. Columns that are frequently used in selective filter operations.

E. Columns that are predominantly utilized in join predicate operations.

Correct Answer: D, E

Explanation: Snowflake emphasizes the strategic use of columns that are recurrently deployed in selective filtering and in join predicate operations to act as clustering keys. By adopting this approach, the system can elevate query performance by ensuring related datasets are located adjacently.

Question-38: Which two crucial objects, when combined, shape a namespace within the Snowflake environment?

A. The user account.

B. The database structure.

C. The schema framework.

D. The table component.

E. The virtual warehouse entity.

Correct Answer: B, C

Explanation: The namespace within Snowflake is architecturally formed by amalgamating a database with a schema. This unique pairing crafts a distinct context for the enclosed objects, thereby facilitating streamlined data management and efficient organization.

Question-39: Keeping the Snowflake data providers in perspective, what's the modus operandi for sharing data that resides in multiple and diverse databases?

A. The creation of external table structures.

B. The deployment of secure views.

C. The formulation of materialized views.

D. The introduction of User-Defined Functions (UDFs).

Correct Answer: B

Explanation: The ingenious use of secure views in Snowflake paves the way for data sharing across various databases. This mechanism ensures that the actual tables remain inaccessible while exposing only the required data to its intended consumers, preserving the sanctity and privacy of data.

Question-40: When uploading a basic CSV file into a Snowflake table with the help of the COPY INTO command, which two tasks can be executed?

A. Running calculations to achieve aggregates.

B. Modifying the sequence of columns.

C. Implementing grouping by operations.

D. Transmuting the inherent data types.

E. Preferring specific rows at the beginning.

Correct Answer: B, D

Explanation: The process of importing a CSV document into Snowflake via the COPY INTO command equips users with the ability to re-arrange columns and transfigure the associated data types. However, tasks such as aggregation, grouping, and selective row operations are beyond the scope of this import function.

Question-41: What are some compelling advantages for a Snowflake user to utilize a secure view? (Select two potential benefits.)

A. It facilitates the retention of non-structured data.

B. It can lead to a noticeable boost in the speed of queries.

C. It provides a mechanism to restrict access to confidential data.

D. It enhances the management of concurrent queries and queuing mechanisms.

E. It shields the specifics and definition of a view from those without proper authorization.

Answer: C,E

Extended **Explanation:** In the Snowflake environment, secure views play a pivotal role in both restricting access to confidential datasets and safeguarding the specifics of a view from those lacking the required permissions. However, they don't inherently aid in storing non-structured data, augmenting query speeds, or refining concurrent query management.

Question-42: In Snowflake's architecture, at which hierarchical levels is it possible to set up a resource monitor? (Select two suitable levels.)

A. On the overall Account tier

B. At the individual Database stage

C. On the Organizational plane

D. Within the Schema layer

E. Pertaining to the Virtual warehouse domain

Answer: A,E

Extended **Explanation:** Within Snowflake's system, resource monitors can be established at the overarching Account tier and in relation to the Virtual warehouse domain. Their primary function is to oversee and govern the utilization of computational resources.

Question-43: What kind of valuable information can a Snowflake user extract from the detailed section of a Query Profile?

A. It offers insights into the total time taken for the query's execution.

B. It reveals the specific role assigned to the user executing the query.

C. It allows identification of the originating system of the queried dataset.

D. It clarifies if the query pertained to structured or semi-structured datasets.

Answer: A

Extended **Explanation:** Snowflake's Query Profile offers a detailed segment that chiefly provides a breakdown regarding the cumulative time duration of the query. This enables users to scrutinize and further enhance their query efficiency.

Question-44: How might a Snowflake user access a JSON object, given the following table structure? (Choose two.)

A. By using src:salesperson.name

B. By using src:salesPerson.name

C. By using src:salesPerson.Name

D. By using SRC:salesPerson.name

E. By using SRC:salesPerson.Name

Correct Answer: B,D

Explanation: In Snowflake, JSON objects can be accessed through case-sensitive dot notation. Therefore, the options src:salesPerson.name and SRC:salesPerson.name can be used to access the JSON object, depending on the original case of the object name.

Question-45: Which data types can be used in a Snowflake table that holds semi-structured data? (Choose two.)

A. ARRAY

B. BINARY

C. TEXT

D. VARIANT

E. VARCHAR

Correct Answer: A,D

Explanation: For tables containing semi-structured data in Snowflake, the data types ARRAY and VARIANT are often used. They are designed to support complex, multi-structured data that may not fit neatly into tabular structures.

Question-46: Which operations are primarily handled within the Cloud Services layer of Snowflake? (Choose two.)

A. Security management

B. Data storage operations

C. Data visualization tasks

D. Query computation tasks

E. Metadata management tasks

Correct Answer: A,E

Explanation: In Snowflake's architecture, the Cloud Services layer is responsible for security and metadata management. Data storage, data visualization, and query computation are handled in other layers of the architecture.

Question-47: Which pieces of statistical information in a Query Profile may suggest that the query is too large to fit in memory? (Choose two.)

A. Bytes spilled to local cache.

B. Bytes spilled to local storage.

C. Bytes spilled to remote cache.

D. Bytes spilled to remote storage.

E. Bytes spilled to remote metastore.

Correct Answer: B,D

Explanation: In Snowflake, if a query is too large to fit in memory, you might notice bytes being spilled to local storage and remote storage. These are signs that the query result set is larger than the available memory, requiring additional storage space.

Question-48: Which commands support a multiple-statement request to access and update Snowflake data? (Choose two.)

A. CALL command

B. COMMIT command

C. GET command

D. PUT command

E. ROLLBACK command

Correct Answer: B,E

Explanation: In Snowflake, the COMMIT and ROLLBACK commands can be used in multiple-statement requests for accessing and updating data. These commands are part of transaction control, allowing you to commit changes or rollback transactions.

Question-49: What types of activities can a user monitor directly from the Activity tab in Snowsight without utilizing the Account_Usage views? (Choose two.)

A. Login history activities

B. Query history activities

C. Copy history activities

D. Event usage history activities

E. Virtual warehouse metering history activities

Correct Answer: B,C

Explanation: The Activity tab in Snowsight provides direct visibility into query history and copy history. It does not provide access to login history, event usage history, or virtual warehouse metering history activities.

Question-50: According to Snowflake's recommendations, what should the Parquet file size be when querying from external tables to optimize the number of parallel scanning operations?

A. 1-16 MB in size

B. 16-128 MB in size

C. 100-250 MB in size

D. 256-512 MB in size

Correct Answer: C

Explanation: For optimal performance when querying from external tables in Snowflake, it is recommended that Parquet files should be within the range of 100-250 MB. This size helps to balance the number of parallel scanning operations, which in turn can improve query performance.

Question-51: Within the framework of Snowflake's data warehousing service, which specific constraint type does the system actively ensure is met?

A. Is it the FOREIGN KEY constraint?

B. Could it be the NOT NULL constraint?

C. Perhaps the PRIMARY KEY constraint?

D. Or the UNIQUE KEY constraint?

Correct Answer: B

Explanation: Within Snowflake, it does not actively enforce constraints such as PRIMARY KEY, FOREIGN KEY, or UNIQUE KEY. However, it does stringently enforce the NOT NULL constraint. If an attempt is made to insert a null value into a column that is earmarked as NOT NULL, Snowflake will promptly reject that operation.

Question-52: In which specific situations might it be advisable for a Snowflake user to turn off the auto-suspend feature for a virtual warehouse? (Choose the best two options.)

A. When compute resources are being accessed unpredictably throughout the day, spanning 24 hours?

B. During the management of a non-stop, continuous workload?

C. When the instantaneous availability of compute resources is paramount, with no room for latency or delays?

D. If the user finds manually initiating the warehouse every time bothersome?

E. When different teams concurrently make use of the warehouse?

Correct Answer: B,C

Explanation: Turning off the auto-suspend feature can be advantageous in cases such as the management of an ongoing, continuous workload (Option B) or when there's a necessity for compute resources to be instantly accessible without any form of delay (Option C). These situations require resources to be instantly available, thereby eliminating the lag that activating from auto-suspend might produce.

Question-53: During the data import procedure in Snowflake, how is data systematically arranged? (Select the best two ways.)

A. Is it arranged into a standard binary format?

B. Does it get organized into a columnar format?

C. Maybe it's transitioned into a compressed format?

D. Could it be maintained in its raw, untouched format?

E. Is it organized into a universally recognized zipped format?

Correct Answer: B,C

Explanation: As data is funneled into Snowflake, it undergoes a transformation into a columnar format (Option B) which is instrumental in boosting query performance by curtailing I/O operations. Additionally, the data is organized into a compressed format (Option C) which is beneficial for optimizing storage utilization.

Question-54: If there's a need for a Snowflake user to disseminate unstructured data from an internal stage to a third-party reporting tool that doesn't inherently support Snowflake, which specific file function would be most apt to use?

A. BUILD_SCOPED_FILE_URL function perhaps?

B. Or the BUILD_STAGE_FILE_URL function?

C. Maybe the GET_PRESIGNED_URL function?

D. What about the GET_STAGE_LOCATION function?

Correct Answer: B

Explanation: In scenarios where there's a need to share data with external services that don't natively communicate with Snowflake, the BUILD_STAGE_FILE_URL function is invaluable. This function is adept at generating a presigned URL that points directly to a file in a specified stage.

Question-55: In the context of efficiently overseeing ETL (Extract, Transform, Load) processes, which kind of Snowflake table could be effectively employed to curtail associated costs?

A. The External table?

B. The Permanent table, maybe?

C. The Temporary table, perhaps?

D. Could it be the Transient table?

Correct Answer: C

Explanation: Temporary tables, as featured in Snowflake, are pivotal in temporarily storing interim results. These tables can be cost-effective since they get discarded post the session's conclusion, ensuring no additional charges for fail-safe storage or historical data preservation.

Question-56: In the context of setting a session policy in Snowflake, which of the following options represents the minimum duration for an idle timeout?

A. A duration of 2 minutes.

B. A span of 5 minutes.

C. A time frame of 10 minutes.

D. An interval of 15 minutes.

Correct Answer: B

Explanation: In Snowflake, when one configures the idle timeout for a session policy, the shortest duration they can select is 5 minutes. If a session remains inactive for this set period, it will be subsequently terminated.

Question-57: When considering the task of momentarily overriding an active network policy using the user object property named MINS_TO_BYPASS_NETWORK_POLICY, which of the following roles or privileges is the absolute minimum requirement?

A. Exclusively when operating under the ACCOUNTADMIN role.

B. Solely when performing actions as the SECURITYADMIN.

C. Only roles possessing the OWNERSHIP privilege over the network policy.

D. This property is exclusively adjustable by Snowflake Support.

Correct Answer: D

Explanation: Setting the MINS_TO_BYPASS_NETWORK_POLICY parameter is a privilege restricted solely to Snowflake Support. This restrictive measure ensures that there aren't any unwarranted alterations to the network policies, thereby maintaining security.

Question-58: In Snowflake, which authentication mechanism is employed by the Kafka connector?

A. The authentication using a public-private key pair.

B. The Multi-Factor Authentication, often referred to as MFA.

C. The OAuth authentication method.

D. The classic Username and Password mechanism.

Correct Answer: A

Explanation: The Kafka connector in Snowflake leans on the key pair authentication method for its operations. This involves the use of a public and private key pairing which guarantees a secure authentication process for the connector.

Question-59: For a Snowflake user aiming to retrieve the URL of a directory table present on an external stage for further transformations, which approach should they adopt?

A. The utilization of the SHOW STAGES command.

B. Engaging the DESCRIBE STAGE command.

C. Resorting to the GET_ABSOLUTE_PATH function.

D. Employing the GET_STAGE_LOCATION function.

Correct Answer: D

Explanation: In Snowflake, the GET_STAGE_LOCATION function is instrumental in acquiring the URL of a directory table located on an external stage. When invoked, this function provides the exact location, be it on Amazon S3, Google Cloud Storage, or even Microsoft Azure.

Question-60: When a user wishes to generate a hosted file URL in Snowflake for a file that has been staged, considering they have both the stage name and the relative file path, which function would be the most appropriate?

A. The function known as BUILD_STAGE_FILE_URL.

B. The function termed as BUILD_SCOPED_FILE_URL.

C. The function called GET_PRESIGNED_URL.

D. The function titled GET_STAGE_LOCATION.

Correct Answer: A

Explanation: Snowflake's BUILD_STAGE_FILE_URL function is designed to produce a URL that points directly to a file situated in a stage. Once generated, this URL grants users the ability to download the staged file directly, making it the optimal choice for this specific task.

Question-61: In relation to semi-structured data formats, which ones among the options support NULL values? Choose two.

A. Avro

B. JSON

C. ORC

D. Parquet

E. SQL

Correct Answer: B, E

Explanation: Semi-structured data is data that doesn't adhere to a rigid structure or format but uses tags to demarcate and establish hierarchies of records and fields. Among the options provided, it is JSON and SQL that support NULL values in this context.

Question-62: Which of the following are true characteristics of transient tables in Snowflake? Select two.

A. Transient tables possess a Fail-safe duration of 7 days.

B. One can clone transient tables to become permanent ones.

C. Transient tables continue to exist until explicitly deleted.

D. There's an option to alter transient tables to make them permanent.

E. Transient tables come with Time Travel retention durations of either 0 or 1 day.

Correct Answer: C, E

Explanation: Transient tables within Snowflake remain in existence until a user explicitly removes them. Moreover, these tables maintain a record of data changes, but only for a very brief span, typically 0 or 1 day.

Question-63: Concerning each database, which items are part of the INFORMATION_SCHEMA? Choose two from the list.

A. Views representing every object housed within the database

B. Views that represent all entities within the Snowflake account

C. Views capturing historical data and usage patterns across the Snowflake account

D. Table functions detailing historical and usage data throughout the Snowflake account

E. Table functions related to account-level entities such as roles, virtual warehouses, and databases

Correct Answer: A, D

Explanation: The INFORMATION_SCHEMA is a standard schema provided by the system. This schema comprises views that detail the objects present in each database. Additionally, it contains table functions that present historical and usage data spanning the Snowflake account.

Question-64: When considering Snowflake's hierarchical key mode, which keys are part of it? Choose two from the options below.

A. Keys for the master account

B. Keys for the master database

C. Keys for individual files

D. Keys for secure viewing

E. Master keys for schemas

Correct Answer: A, C

Explanation: Within the hierarchical key mode in Snowflake, the account master keys and file keys play a pivotal role. These keys are integral to the processes of encryption and decryption, ensuring the safety of data.

Question-65: Which statement accurately describes a feature of Snowflake's materialized views?

A. Materialized views in Snowflake restrict the use of joins.

B. Users can directly generate clones from materialized views.

C. In a materialized view's foundational query, you can join multiple tables.

D. In materialized views, aggregate functions can act as window functions.

Correct Answer: A

Explanation: One notable feature of Snowflake's materialized views is that they do not support the use of joins. This implies that within a materialized view, combining rows from multiple tables based on related columns isn't possible.

Question-66: To facilitate a request and data reception by a consumer in the Data Exchange, what privileges must be held? (Choose two from the options provided.)

A. CREATE DATABASE

B. IMPORT SHARE

C. OWNERSHIP

D. REFERENCE_USAGE

E. USAGE

Correct Answer: A,B

Explanation: For a consumer to successfully initiate requests and receive data within the Data Exchange platform, the necessary privileges include 'CREATE DATABASE' and 'IMPORT SHARE'. These specific privileges enable the consumer to establish new databases and import shared data, respectively.

Question-67: What term is employed to depict the details concerning disk utilization for operations when intermediate outcomes surpass the capacity of a Snowflake virtual warehouse's memory?

A. Pruning

B. Spilling

C. Join explosion

D. Queue overloading

Correct Answer: B

Explanation: The precise term that characterizes this scenario is 'Spilling'. When intermediate results exceed the available memory capacity in a Snowflake virtual warehouse, the data is 'spilled' or stored on disk. This maneuver permits the operation to proceed without hindrance.

Question-68: When confronted with the task of transferring data from a production Snowflake account to a non-production account within the same cloud provider region, what approach ensures seamless data transfer?

A. Duplicate the data from the production account to the non-production account through cloning.

B. Establish a data share, facilitating data transfer from the production account to the non-production account.

C. Generate a subscription within the production account and set it to publish data to the non-production account.

D. Formulate a reader account within the production account, subsequently linking it to the non-production account.

Correct Answer: A

Explanation: The process of cloning is a proficient method for seamlessly moving data between Snowflake accounts situated within the same cloud provider region. This technique involves creating a copy of data originating from the source, which in this context is the production account, and transmitting it to the target account, namely the non-production account.

Question-69: A user executes the following command to unload data to a designated stage: copy into @message from (select object_construct('id', 1, 'first_name', 'Snowflake', 'last_name', 'User', 'city', 'Bozeman')) file_format = (type = json). What format will the output file in the designated stage assume?

A. A solitary compressed JSON file incorporating a single VARIANT column

B. Numerous compressed JSON files containing a single VARIANT column each

C. A lone uncompressed JSON file housing multiple VARIANT columns

D. Several uncompressed JSON files each accommodating multiple VARIANT columns

Correct Answer: A

Explanation: The provided command execution results in the generation of a solitary compressed JSON file featuring a single VARIANT column. The utilization of the object_construct function constructs a JSON object employing the provided parameters, subsequently transferring it to a file characterized by the JSON format.

Question-70: When dealing with a JSON file encompassing an abundance of dates and arrays necessitating processing in Snowflake, what strategy optimizes query performance?

A. Flatten the data and store it within structured data types within a flattened table, subsequently executing queries on the table.

B. Store the data in a table equipped with a VARIANT data type, thereafter conducting queries on the table.

C. Save the data within a table configured with a VARIANT data type, and include the STRIP_NULL_VALUES attribute during the table loading process. Execute queries on the table.

D. Deposit the data within an external stage, subsequently erecting views atop it. Engage in querying the established views.

Correct Answer: A

Explanation: To ensure optimal querying performance in Snowflake, especially when dealing with data encompassing an extensive array of dates and arrays, the recommended approach is to flatten the data and house it within structured data types located within a flattened table. This technique streamlines the data structure, minimizes complexity, and significantly boosts query performance.

Question-71: Within the realm of Snowflake's User-Defined Function (UDF) nomenclature, what does the term 'overloading' signify?

A. The coexistence of multiple SQL UDFs boasting identical names and the same quantity of arguments.

B. The existence of multiple SQL UDFs sharing the same names and equivalent argument types.

C. The presence of several SQL UDFs sharing identical names while diverging in the count or types of arguments.

D. The availability of multiple SQL UDFs with distinct names, each accompanied by an identical count of arguments or argument types.

Correct Answer: C

Explanation: In the context of Snowflake's User-Defined Functions (UDF), 'overloading' refers to the scenario where multiple SQL UDFs share a common name, yet they differ in the quantity or types of arguments they accept. This flexibility enhances the versatility and applicability of the functions.

Question-72: Within Snowflake's governance framework, which functionality enables the identification of data elements containing sensitive information, along with their associated attributes?

A. Is it the Object Tagging feature?

B. Or could it be Data Classification?

C. Perhaps, is it the Row Access Policy?

D. Or the feature for Column-level Security?

Correct Answer: A

Explanation: In the context of Snowflake's governance framework, the functionality responsible for pinpointing data elements containing sensitive information and their corresponding attributes is the 'Object Tagging' feature. This tool allows for categorization and oversight of data objects, particularly those housing sensitive data. It aids in adhering to data governance principles by flagging objects subject to specific access protocols.

Question-73: What capability does a user possess within Snowflake's administrative sphere?

A. The authority to scrutinize query performance?

B. The capacity to formulate and execute queries?

C. An extensive view of offerings within the Snowflake Marketplace?

D. The ability to connect with Snowflake partners to explore supplementary features?

Correct Answer: D

Explanation: Within Snowflake's administrative domain, users are equipped with the ability to establish connections with Snowflake partners, affording them access to extended functionalities. This capability proves beneficial when users seek to harness additional features or capabilities that may extend beyond the core Snowflake offerings.

Question-74: What constitutes the primary objective behind the utilization of the OBJECT_CONSTRUCT function in conjunction with the COPY INTO command?

A. Is it the rearrangement of rows within a relational table, followed by their subsequent unloading into a file?

B. Or is it the conversion of rows within a relational table into a single VARIANT column, subsequently unloaded into a file?

C. Does it involve reordering data columns to align with a target table's definition, followed by the unloading of rows into the table?

D. Perhaps it entails the transformation of rows within a source file into a solitary VARIANT column, then loading the rows from the file into a variant table?

Correct Answer: B

Explanation: The primary purpose of deploying the OBJECT_CONSTRUCT function alongside the COPY INTO command is to convert the rows present within a relational table into a single VARIANT column. Subsequently, these transformed rows are unloaded into a file. The VARIANT data type, specific to Snowflake, is adept at handling semi-structured data formats like JSON, Avro, ORC, Parquet, or XML.

Question-75: Which type of URL facilitates access to files within Snowflake devoid of requiring explicit authentication?

A. Is it the File URL?

B. Or possibly, the Scoped URL?

C. Could it be the Pre-signed URL?

D. Or perhaps the Scoped file URL?

Correct Answer: C

Explanation: The mechanism that provides an avenue for accessing files within Snowflake without necessitating additional authentication is the 'Pre-signed URL'. These URLs are signed using the access credentials of the storage account, granting users temporary access to specific files for a predefined duration.

Question-76: How can the performance of Snowflake queries on large tables be significantly improved?

A. Is it through the application of Indexing?

B. Could it be accomplished using Clustering keys?

C. Perhaps Multi-clustering plays a role?

D. Or is the answer Materialized Views?

Correct Answer: B

Explanation: Clustering keys play a vital role in enhancing the performance of Snowflake queries on large tables. By physically organizing the data in a table based on the clustering keys, the amount of data that needs to be scanned for a query is reduced, resulting in improved query performance.

Question-77: Which specific layer within Snowflake's architecture is associated with virtual warehouses?

A. Is it the Cloud Services layer?

B. How about the Query Processing layer?

C. Could it be the Elastic Memory layer?

D. Or is it the Database Storage layer?

Correct Answer: B

Explanation: Virtual Warehouses in Snowflake are closely tied to the Query Processing layer. These virtual warehouses function as Massively Parallel Processing (MPP) compute clusters, enabling the execution of queries and data manipulation operations.

Question-78: What SQL command should be used to download data files from an internal table stage named TBL_EMPLOYEE to a local Windows directory, specifically within a folder named "folder with space" on the C drive?

A. Is it GET @%TBL_EMPLOYEE 'file://C:\folder with space\'?

B. Or maybe GET @%TBL_EMPLOYEE 'file://C:/folder with space/'?

C. Could it be PUT 'file://C:\folder with space*' @%TBL_EMPLOYEE?

D. Or is it PUT 'file://C:/folder with space/*' @%TBL_EMPLOYEE?

Correct Answer: A

Explanation: In this scenario, the correct SQL command is GET @%TBL_EMPLOYEE 'file://C:\folder with space\'. The GET command facilitates the download of data files from an internal stage, while the PUT command is used for file uploads.

Question-79: What primary function does the Snowflake SPLIT_TO_TABLE procedure serve?

A. Is it geared towards counting characters in a string?

B. Or is its purpose to dissect a string into substrings within an array?

C. Perhaps it's focused on splitting a string and presenting the results as rows?

D. Maybe its role involves splitting a string and distributing the results as columns?

Correct Answer: C

Explanation: The chief purpose of the Snowflake SPLIT_TO_TABLE function is to split a string and represent the results as individual rows. This function is particularly useful for dividing a string based on a specified delimiter and presenting each separated value as its own row.

Question-80: Within Snowflake's Continuous Data Protection mechanism, which aspect aids in preserving historical data?

A. Is it Access Control?

B. Could it be Fail-safe?

C. Or maybe Network Policies?

D. Or is it Time Travel?

Correct Answer: D

Explanation: The Time Travel feature within Snowflake's Continuous Data Protection mechanism facilitates the preservation of historical data. This feature allows users to query data at various points within a defined time frame, up to 90 days in the past, making it a valuable tool for maintaining and exploring historical data.

Question-81: What specific aspect of an executed query does the remote disk I/O statistic in the Query Profile reflect?

A. The time spent scanning table partitions to filter data based on predicates

B. The duration dedicated to caching data to remote storage for buffering during extraction and export

C. The time allocated for reading and writing data to remote storage when virtual warehouse memory is insufficient

D. The time taken for reading and writing data to remote storage when accessed data surpasses virtual warehouse memory and local disk capacity

Correct Answer: D

Explanation: The remote disk I/O statistic in the Query Profile pertains to the time taken for reading and writing data to remote storage when accessed data exceeds the capacity of both the virtual warehouse memory and the local disk. This typically occurs when dealing with large data volumes that cannot be entirely stored in memory.

Question-82: What action could mitigate issues related to query concurrency in Snowflake?

A. Activating the search optimization service

B. Enabling the query acceleration service

C. Adding more clusters to the virtual warehouse

D. Upgrading the virtual warehouse to a larger instance size

Correct Answer: C

Explanation: To address query concurrency challenges, one effective approach is to incorporate additional clusters into the virtual warehouse. By increasing the number of clusters, more computational resources are available, allowing multiple queries to run concurrently without performance degradation.

Question-83: What function does the client redirect feature in Snowflake fulfill?

A. Rerouting client connections to Snowflake accounts within the same regions for continuity

B. Redirecting client connections to Snowflake accounts in different regions for continuity

C. Enabling client connections to Snowflake accounts in various regions for data replication

D. Facilitating client connections redirection to Snowflake accounts within the same regions for data replication

Correct Answer: B

Explanation: The client redirect feature in Snowflake enables the redirection of client connections to Snowflake accounts in different regions. This capability ensures continuous service even during regional outages, safeguarding business operations.

Question-84: Which Snowflake feature aids in identifying sensitive data within a table or column?

A. Masking policies

B. Data classification

C. Row-level policies

D. External functions

Correct Answer: B

Explanation: Data classification within Snowflake is employed to detect sensitive data within a table or column. By analyzing and categorizing data based on content and type, this feature assists in identifying sensitive or private information.

Question-85: Which Snowflake feature empowers users to monitor sensitive data concerning compliance, discovery, protection, and resource usage?

A. Tags

B. Comments

C. Internal tokenization

D. Row access policies

Correct Answer: A

Explanation: The tags feature in Snowflake empowers users to track sensitive data for purposes such as compliance, discovery, protection, and resource management. Tags can be applied to Snowflake objects to aid in categorization and management.

Question-86: What can be managed using the Snowflake SCIM API? (Choose two.)

A. Integrations

B. Network policies

C. Session policies

D. Roles

E. Users

Correct Answer: D, E

Explanation: The Snowflake System for Cross-domain Identity Management (SCIM) API is used for managing roles and users. This API offers a standardized mechanism for automating the provisioning and de-provisioning of users and roles, along with their attributes.

Question-87: What privilege is required to utilize Snowflake's search optimization service?

A. GRANT SEARCH OPTIMIZATION ON SCHEMA TO ROLE

B. GRANT SEARCH OPTIMIZATION ON DATABASE TO ROLE

C. GRANT ADD SEARCH OPTIMIZATION ON SCHEMA TO ROLE

D. GRANT ADD SEARCH OPTIMIZATION ON DATABASE TO ROLE

Correct Answer: C

Explanation: To utilize the search optimization service in Snowflake, the privilege 'GRANT ADD SEARCH OPTIMIZATION ON SCHEMA TO ROLE' is essential. This permission allows a specified role to add a search optimization service to a schema.

Question-88: Generally, what method is considered the most expedient for bulk loading data files from a stage in Snowflake?

A. Providing a list of specific files for loading

B. Loading by path (internal stages) / prefix

C. Utilizing the Snowpipe REST API

D. Using pattern matching to identify specific files based on a pattern

Correct Answer: A

Explanation: In most cases, specifying a list of specific files for loading is the fastest approach for bulk loading data files from a stage in Snowflake. This method enables parallel processing and significantly speeds up data loading.

Question-89: What characteristic applies to Snowflake data shares?

A. Data shares support complete DML operations

B. Data shares involve copying data to consumer accounts

C. Data shares use secure views for sharing view objects

D. Data shares are cloud-agnostic and inherently span regions

Correct Answer: C

Explanation: Data shares within Snowflake employ secure views to share view objects. This approach ensures that only the outcome of the view query is shared, preserving the confidentiality of underlying data. It's a secure way to share data.

Question-90: Which command is used to unload data from a Snowflake table to an external stage?

A. COPY INTO

B. COPY INTO followed by GET

C. GET

D. COPY INTO followed by PUT

Correct Answer: A

Explanation: The 'COPY INTO' command is employed to unload data from a Snowflake table to an external stage. This command copies the outcome of a SELECT statement (which can originate from a table) to files within a stage.

Question-91: What type of Snowflake URL enables users or applications to access or download files directly from a Snowflake stage without requiring authentication?

A. Directory

B. File

C. Pre-signed

D. Scoped

Correct Answer: C

Explanation: The pre-signed URL type in Snowflake allows users or applications to access files from a Snowflake stage without authentication. This is particularly useful for accessing Snowflake data from external services or applications that may lack direct authentication capabilities.

Question-92: Which method can be utilized through the COPY command to move data from a table to an internal stage?

A. The 'COPY INTO' statement

B. The 'COPY INTO' statement with single-true

C. 'COPY INTO' directed at 'S3://'

D. 'COPY INTO' coupled with multiple-UDFs

Correct Answer: A, B

Explanation: To unload data from a table to an internal stage, the 'COPY INTO' command can be used. It is a versatile Snowflake command that facilitates copying query results into tables or internal stages. This aids in efficiently handling large datasets.

Question-93: When comparing a Snowflake stored procedure to a User-Defined Function (UDF), what observation can be made?

A. A single executable statement can call just one stored procedure, whereas numerous UDFs can be invoked by a single SQL statement.

B. Multiple stored procedures can be summoned by a single executable statement, whereas the same UDF can be called by multiple SQL statements.

C. Only two stored procedures can be invoked by a single executable statement, while a single SQL statement can utilize multiple UDFs.

D. More than one stored procedure can be summoned by numerous executable statements, whereas a single SQL statement can invoke multiple UDFs.

Correct Answer: A

Explanation: A key distinction between a Snowflake stored procedure and a User-Defined Function (UDF) is that a single executable statement can invoke just one stored procedure.

In contrast, a single SQL statement has the capability to call upon multiple UDFs. This distinction influences application development and data processing tasks.

Question-94: Which command is essential to unload all rows from a table into one or more files in a designated stage?

A. COPY INTO

B. GET

C. INSERT INTO

D. PUT

Correct Answer: A

Explanation: The 'COPY INTO' command in Snowflake is used to unload all rows from a table and store them in one or more files within a designated stage. This command efficiently extracts query results and moves them into tables or internal stages, particularly useful for managing substantial data volumes.

Question-95: Which command Is employed to unload data from a table or transfer a query result to a stage?

A. COPY INTO

B. GET

C. MERGE

D. PUT

Correct Answer: A

Explanation: The 'COPY INTO' command is employed in Snowflake to unload data from a table or transfer the result of a query to a stage. This command is powerful and versatile, assisting in managing large datasets by moving them to stages for further processing or storage.

Question-96: What are the advantages of using Snowpark in conjunction with Snowflake? (Choose two.)

A. Snowpark employs a Spark engine to optimize SQL query plans.

B. Snowpark sets up Spark automatically within Snowflake virtual warehouses.

C. Snowpark eliminates the need for an external cluster outside of Snowflake.

D. Snowpark allows execution of existing Spark code on virtual warehouses without reconfiguration.

E. Snowpark offloads as much work as possible to source databases, including User-Defined Functions (UDFs).

Correct Answer: C, D

Explanation: Utilizing Snowpark with Snowflake provides benefits such as not requiring an external cluster outside of Snowflake, simplifying the data environment. Additionally, Snowpark enables executing existing Spark code on virtual warehouses without requiring code reconfiguration, enhancing efficiency and productivity.

Question-97: What are the recommended practices in Snowflake for assigning the ACCOUNTADMIN role to users? (Choose two.)

A. Assign the ACCOUNTADMIN role to at least two users.

B. Utilize the ACCOUNTADMIN role for creating Snowflake objects.

C. Run automated scripts using the ACCOUNTADMIN role.

D. Grant the ACCOUNTADMIN role to users needing high authority.

E. Ensure users assigned the ACCOUNTADMIN role use Multi-Factor Authentication (MFA).

Correct Answer: A, E

Explanation: Best practices for assigning the ACCOUNTADMIN role in Snowflake include assigning it to at least two users to prevent administrative access loss due to unforeseen issues. Furthermore, for enhanced security, all users with the ACCOUNTADMIN role should implement Multi-Factor Authentication (MFA) to provide an extra layer of protection.

Question-98: What is a recommended strategy for optimizing query performance in Snowflake?

A. Maximize the usage of subqueries.

B. Increase the number of joins to combine data from multiple tables.

C. Select all available columns from tables, regardless of query requirements.

D. Opt for fewer large tables rather than numerous small tables.

Correct Answer: D

Explanation: To optimize query performance in Snowflake, it's advisable to opt for fewer large tables over many small tables. This approach reduces the number of I/O operations, leading to improved query performance. Snowflake is designed to efficiently manage large tables, and utilizing fewer large tables simplifies data modeling and query complexity.

Question-99: Which configuration options are necessary when unloading data from a SQL query executed on a local machine using SnowSQL? (Choose two.)

A. echo

B. quiet

C. output_file

D. output_format

E. force_put_overwrite

Correct Answer: C, D

Explanation: When unloading data from a SQL query executed using SnowSQL on a local machine, the required configuration options are 'output_file' and 'output_format'. 'output_file' specifies the destination file for the unloaded data, while 'output_format' determines the output data format, such as CSV or JSON.

Question-100: Which Snowflake view is designed to facilitate compliance auditing?

A. ACCESS_HISTORY

B. COPY_HISTORY

C. QUERY_HISTORY

D. ROW_ACCESS_POLICIES

Correct Answer: A

Explanation: The 'ACCESS_HISTORY' view in Snowflake is dedicated to supporting compliance auditing. This view offers insights into access attempts made to Snowflake objects, providing essential data for auditing and security purposes. It records details of access attempts, including who attempted access, when, and the success status.

SnowPro Practice Paper-2

Question-1: How can a user effectively manage loading files with duplicates in the Snowflake environment using the COPY INTO command?

A. Adjust the COPY INTO settings with PURGE set to FALSE

B. Adjust the COPY INTO settings with FORCE set to TRUE

C. Adjust the COPY INTO settings with RETURN_FAILED_ONLY set to FALSE

D. Adjust the COPY INTO settings with ON_ERROR set to CONTINUE

Correct Answer: B

Explanation: To handle duplicate files when using the COPY INTO command, the user should adjust the settings by setting the FORCE option to TRUE. This allows Snowflake to forcefully load the data, bypassing duplicate constraints and enabling the loading of duplicate files.

Question-2: What scenario could result in the objects within a data share becoming inaccessible to a consumer account?

A. Setting the DATA_RETENTION_TIME_IN_DAYS parameter in the consumer account to 0.

B. Executing the GRANT IMPORTED PRIVILEGES command on the data share every 24 hours in the consumer account.

C. Deleting the objects within the data share and neglecting to consistently reapply the grant pattern.

D. Acquiring the data share through a private data exchange by the consumer account.

Correct Answer: C

Explanation: Objects within a data share could become inaccessible to a consumer account if they are deleted and the grant pattern is not regularly reapplied. The grant pattern is crucial for granting access to the consumer account, and failing to reapply it would lead to inaccessibility.

Question-3: How are Snowflake tables typically defined in terms of their nature?

A. Snowflake tables serve as logical representations of the underlying physical data.

B. Snowflake tables embody the physical data loaded into Snowflake.

C. Snowflake tables exhibit optimal performance only with defined clustering keys.

D. Snowflake tables are possessed by specific user accounts.

Correct Answer: A

Explanation: Snowflake tables are essentially logical representations of the underlying physical data stored within Snowflake. Users interact with these tables to work with the data, while Snowflake manages the physical data storage and retrieval.

Question-4: Which types of visualizations are supported by Snowsight? (Select two.)

A. Flowcharts

B. Gantt charts

C. Line charts

D. Pie charts

E. Scatterplots

Correct Answer: C, D

Explanation: Snowsight, the visualization tool offered by Snowflake, supports various visualization types, including line charts and pie charts. These visualization options are valuable for effectively conveying insights derived from data.

Question-5: For uploading a file to an internal Snowflake stage using a PUT command, which tools or connectors are suitable for executing this command? (Select two.)

A. SnowCD

B. SnowSQL

C. SQL API

D. Python connector

E. Snowsight worksheets

Correct Answer: B, D

Explanation: To execute a PUT command in Snowflake, users can utilize either the SnowSQL command-line tool or the Python connector. Both of these options allow the execution of Snowflake SQL commands, including the PUT command for uploading files.

Question-6: What type of Snowflake table is associated with a stage, regardless of whether the stage is internal or external?

A. Directory table

B. Temporary table

C. Transient table

D. Table with a materialized view

Correct Answer: A

Explanation: In Snowflake, a directory table is implicitly linked to a stage, whether the stage is internal or external. This table enables users to query the metadata of files present in the stage.

Question-7: Which Snowflake account usage view is particularly useful for identifying the most frequently accessed tables?

A. Access_History

B. Object_Dependencies

C. Table_Storage_Metrics

D. Tables

Correct Answer: A

Explanation: The Access_History account usage view in Snowflake is employed to monitor the utilization of various database objects. It is specifically valuable for identifying the tables that experience the highest frequency of access.

Question-8: Based on the provided Query Profile image for a Snowsight query, featuring four highlighted nodes in yellow, which of these highlighted nodes would likely have the highest associated cost?

A. Aggregate[1]

B. Join[5]

C. TableScan[2]

D. TableScan[3]

Correct Answer: D

Explanation: While the specific image is not provided, generally, the cost of a TableScan operation is determined by the number of rows and columns involved. If TableScan[3] is identified as the most costly node, it indicates that it is scanning a larger portion of data compared to the other operations.

Question-9: What stands as a distinctive feature of maintaining a materialized view within Snowflake?

A. Materialized views cannot be automatically refreshed.

B. Additional scripts are necessary for refreshing data in materialized views.

C. Snowflake's managed warehouse refreshes a materialized view automatically.

D. A materialized view can be configured for auto-refresh using the SQL SET command.

Correct Answer: C

Explanation: In Snowflake, a materialized view is automatically maintained by the system. Whenever data changes that impact the results of the materialized view query are committed, Snowflake updates the materialized view automatically.

Question-10: Which command should be utilized to implement a pre-established masking policy in Snowflake?

A. ALTER MASKING POLICY

B. APPLY MASKING POLICY

C. CREATE MASKING POLICY

D. SET MASKING POLICY

Correct Answer: B

Explanation: After creating a masking policy in Snowflake, the 'APPLY MASKING POLICY' command is used to enforce the policy on a specific column within a table. This ensures that the data in the column is masked according to the rules defined in the policy.

Question-11: Which command facilitates the process of unloading all rows from a table into files located within a named stage in Snowflake?

A. COPY INTO

B. GET

C. INSERT INTO

D. PUT

Correct Answer: A

Explanation: The COPY INTO command in Snowflake is employed to extract data from a table and store it within files located in a specified stage. This capability is particularly useful for efficiently moving significant amounts of data.

Question-12: Among the provided statements, which accurately portrays a characteristic of materialized views?

A. A materialized view can solely query a single table.

B. Data accessed through materialized views may occasionally be outdated.

C. Maintenance of a materialized view's refreshes requires user intervention.

D. Querying a materialized view is slower compared to executing a query against the base table of the view.

Correct Answer: B

Explanation: This statement is accurate. Materialized views can store results from complex queries involving multiple tables. However, the data in a materialized view can become outdated if the underlying data changes are not automatically reflected in the view.

Question-13: Which Snowflake table type is commonly employed to reduce costs associated with ETL workflows?

A. External

B. Permanent

C. Temporary

D. Transient

Correct Answer: C

Explanation: Temporary tables in Snowflake are particularly suitable for ETL workflows. They exist only within the session in which they were created and are automatically dropped when the session ends. This reduces storage costs as these tables do not persist beyond the active session.

Question-14: To unload data from a relational table into a CSV file within an external stage, with the file name aligned exactly as specified by the user, which file format option is mandatory?

A. encoding

B. escape

C. file_extension

D. single

Correct Answer: C

Explanation: In this scenario, the 'file_extension' option must be used. It allows the user to specify the extension of the output file, which in this case would be a CSV file.

Question-15: Among the provided objects, which ones can be cloned within Snowflake? (Select four.)

A. Tables

B. Named File Formats

C. Schemas

D. Shares

E. Databases

F. Users

Correct Answer: A, B, C, E

Explanation: In Snowflake, Tables, Named File Formats, Schemas, and Databases can be cloned, allowing for the efficient replication of these objects. However, Shares and Users cannot be cloned.

Question-16: Why might a customer decide to transition a Virtual Warehouse from an X-Small size to a Medium size?

A. To accommodate an increased number of queries

B. To accommodate a higher number of users

C. To handle variations in workload

D. To manage a more intricate workload

Correct Answer: D

Explanation: Scaling up a Virtual Warehouse to a larger size, like Medium, grants access to greater computational resources, enabling faster processing of more intricate workloads. Hence, customers might opt to switch from an X-Small to a Medium Virtual Warehouse to handle more complex workloads effectively.

Question-17: Which statements regarding Virtual Warehouses hold true? (Select all that apply.)

A. Customers can modify the Warehouse size after its creation

B. Resizing a Warehouse is feasible even when it is operational

C. A Warehouse can be set to suspend after a period of inactivity

D. A Warehouse can be configured to auto-resume upon new query submissions

Correct Answer: A, B

Explanation: A and B are accurate. Customers can adjust a Virtual Warehouse's size post-creation and can also alter the size while it's actively running. However, it is not mandatory for a Warehouse to be set to suspend due to inactivity or to automatically resume when new queries are submitted; these behaviors depend on user-defined settings.

Question-18: Given a deterministic query executed at 8am, taking 5 minutes with cached results, which assertions are correct? (Choose two.)

A. The exact same query will ALWAYS retrieve the precomputed results within the RESULT_CACHE_ACTIVE time frame.

B. If the underlying data remains unchanged and results were accessed in the past 24 hours, the query will consistently yield precomputed results.

C. Regardless of underlying data changes, the same query will produce cached results as long as they were last accessed in the previous 24 hours.

D. The "24-hour" timer for precomputed results restarts with every execution of the exact query.

Correct Answer: B, D

Explanation: Statement B is accurate because Snowflake supports result caching; unchanged data yields consistent precomputed results within 24 hours. Statement D is also true; the timer for cached results resets each time the query is executed.

Question-19: What assertions about Snowflake releases are valid? (Choose two.)

A. Releases occur roughly on a weekly basis

B. Releases are consolidated and issued approximately monthly, but users can request early application

C. During a release, new customer activities automatically shift to the newer version

D. Users are assigned a 30-minute upgrade window, movable within a week, during which the system is inaccessible for upgrades

Correct Answer: A, C

Explanation: Statement A holds true, as Snowflake generally conducts weekly maintenance and releases. Statement C is also accurate; Snowflake seamlessly upgrades by migrating customer activities to the new version during releases.

Question-20: Which interfaces are usable for the creation and management of Virtual Warehouses?

A. The Snowflake Web Interface (UI)

B. SQL commands

C. Data integration tools

D. All of the above

Correct Answer: D

Explanation: All the mentioned interfaces—Snowflake web interface, SQL commands, and various data integration tools—can be employed to create and manage Virtual Warehouses within Snowflake.

Question-21: When it comes to establishing and overseeing users and roles in Snowflake, which role is typically recommended for this purpose?

A. SYSADMIN

B. SECURITYADMIN

C. PUBLIC

D. ACCOUNTADMIN

Correct Answer: B

Explanation: The role of SECURITYADMIN is specifically designed for the task of creating and managing users and roles in Snowflake. This role is equipped with the necessary privileges and is, therefore, the recommended choice for performing these actions.

Question-22: Verify the accuracy of the following statement: The process of bulk unloading data from Snowflake indeed supports the usage of a SELECT statement.

A. Confirm (True)

B. Deny (False)

Correct Answer: A

Explanation: This statement is true. The bulk unloading process in Snowflake indeed allows the usage of a SELECT statement. This enables users to define and select specific datasets for unloading.

Question-23: Which factors influence credit consumption in the Compute Layer (Virtual Warehouses)? (Choose two.)

A. Number of users

B. Warehouse size

C. Volume of data processed

D. Number of clusters for the Warehouse

Correct Answer: B, D

Explanation: Credit consumption in Snowflake's Compute Layer primarily hinges on the size of the warehouse and the number of clusters engaged. A larger warehouse and a greater number of clusters lead to higher consumption of computational resources and, consequently, more credits.

Question-24: Can you confirm or refute the following statement: The COPY command in Snowflake requires the specification of a File Format for execution.

A. Confirm (True)

B. Deny (False)

Correct Answer: B

Explanation: This statement is false. The COPY command does not necessarily require an explicit File Format specification to execute. If no file format is indicated, Snowflake resorts to the default file format.

Question-25: Which of the following statements aptly outline the benefits of Snowflake's segregation of compute and storage? (Choose all that apply.)

A. Expansion of storage and compute are intricately linked

B. Storage can expand without necessitating additional compute resources

C. Compute can be dynamically adjusted without the need for extra storage

D. Multiple compute clusters can access stored data concurrently without conflicts

Correct Answer: B, C, D

Explanation: The segregation of compute and storage in Snowflake facilitates independent scaling. As a result, storage can grow without requiring more compute resources (B), compute can be scaled up or down without affecting storage (C), and multiple compute clusters can access stored data simultaneously without contention (D).

Question-26: Please affirm or refute the following statement: Snowflake's data warehouse was purpose-built for the cloud, rather than being adapted from an existing database or platform like Hadoop.

A. Confirm (True)

B. Deny (False)

Correct Answer: A

Explanation: This statement is true. Snowflake's data warehouse is entirely native to the cloud. It was designed from the ground up specifically for cloud usage, as opposed to being derived from an existing database or platform like Hadoop.

Question-27: What occurs when a Pipe is recreated using the CREATE OR REPLACE PIPE command in Snowflake?

A. The Pipe's load history is reset to empty

B. The REFRESH parameter is set to TRUE

C. Previously loaded files are disregarded

D. All of the above

Correct Answer: A

Explanation: When a Pipe is recreated using the CREATE OR REPLACE PIPE command in Snowflake, the Pipe's load history is reset to empty. This action erases the historical record of all files previously loaded through the Pipe.

Question-28: For customers aiming to store sensitive information in Snowflake while ensuring regulatory adherence, what is the minimum Snowflake edition to consider?

A. Standard

B. Premier

C. Enterprise

D. Business Critical Edition

Correct Answer: D

Explanation: The Business Critical Edition of Snowflake is the minimum edition suitable for storing protected information. This edition incorporates essential features like customer-managed keys and HIPAA compliance, crucial for safeguarding data and adhering to regulations.

Question-29: What does increasing the maximum number of clusters in a Multi-Cluster Warehouse in Snowflake represent?

A. Gradual scaling

B. Maximum scaling

C. Horizontal scaling

D. Vertical scaling

Correct Answer: C

Explanation: Increasing the maximum number of clusters in a Multi-Cluster Warehouse exemplifies 'horizontal scaling'. This procedure enhances concurrent processing by adding more clusters, effectively distributing the workload across multiple resources.

Question-30: Can you confirm or refute the following statement: Snowflake imposes extra charges on Data Providers for each Share they generate.

A. Confirm (True)

B. Deny (False)

Correct Answer: B

Explanation: This statement is false. Snowflake does not levy additional fees for creating Shares. Shares facilitate data sharing within Snowflake and their creation does not entail supplementary costs.

Question-31: When can a Virtual Warehouse begin executing queries within Snowflake?

A. From 12am to 5am

B. Only during time slots defined by administrators

C. After its provisioning process is completed

D. After data replication

Correct Answer: C

Explanation: A Virtual Warehouse in Snowflake becomes capable of running queries once its provisioning process is finished. Provisioning involves the setup of essential resources and configurations required for the warehouse's functioning. Only after this process is concluded can the warehouse execute queries effectively.

Question-32: In a multi-cluster Warehouse, is it mandatory for users to specify the cluster on which a query should run?

A. Users must specify the cluster each time.

B. Specifying the cluster is unnecessary for users.

C. Only for the initial query, specifying the cluster is required.

D. Users need to specify the cluster when more than three clusters are available.

Correct Answer: B

Explanation: Snowflake's architecture facilitates the automatic distribution of queries across all clusters within a multi-cluster warehouse. Users do not need to manually designate a specific cluster for query execution. This feature ensures seamless and automatic scaling along with load balancing.

Question-33: Can the operation of Pipes be paused and later resumed in Snowflake?

A. Pipes can be paused but not resumed.

B. Pipes can be resumed but not paused.

C. Both pausing and resuming operations are possible for Pipes.

D. Neither pausing nor resuming operations can be done for Pipes.

Correct Answer: C

Explanation: In Snowflake, Pipes offer a robust functionality for streaming data from files into tables. These Pipes can indeed be both paused and resumed according to operational requirements, granting users enhanced flexibility and control.

Question-34: How can Snowflake customers override its natural clustering algorithms?

A. By implementing micro-partitions.

B. By defining clustering keys.

C. By dividing data into key partitions.

D. By creating clustered partitions.

Correct Answer: B

Explanation: Snowflake provides customers with the ability to define clustering keys to override the platform's default clustering algorithms. These keys allow users to manually control data grouping and sorting, thereby enhancing query performance.

Question-35: Which are valid Snowflake Virtual Warehouse Scaling Policies? (Select two.)

A. Custom scaling policy.

B. Economy scaling policy.

C. Optimized scaling policy.

D. Standard scaling policy.

Correct Answer: B, D

Explanation: Valid Snowflake Virtual Warehouse Scaling Policies include Economy and Standard. The Standard policy automatically suspends the warehouse when idle and resumes upon query submission. The Economy policy maximizes cost savings by minimizing compute resources utilized by the warehouse.

Question-36: Is it possible for a single database to exist in multiple Snowflake accounts?

A. A single database can exist in unlimited Snowflake accounts.

B. A single database can only exist in one Snowflake account.

C. A single database can exist in a maximum of two Snowflake accounts.

D. A single database can exist in three Snowflake accounts.

Correct Answer: B

Explanation: In Snowflake, a database is specific to the account within which it's created. It doesn't span across multiple Snowflake accounts.

Question-37: Identify the types of Internal Stages in Snowflake: (Select three.)

A. The Named Stage.

B. The User Stage.

C. The Table Stage.

D. The Schema Stage.

Correct Answer: A, B, C

Explanation: Snowflake Internal Stages are temporary storage areas for staging data files during loading and unloading processes. The types of Internal Stages include Named Stages, User Stages, and Table Stages. There is no such type as Schema Stage in Snowflake.

Question-38: Which types of tables are present in Snowflake? (Select three.)

A. Temporary tables.

B. Transient tables.

C. Provisional tables.

D. Permanent tables.

Correct Answer: A, B, D

Explanation: Snowflake supports three table types: Temporary, Transient, and Permanent. Temporary tables are session-specific and get removed after the session. Transient tables persist beyond the session but may be purged under certain conditions. Permanent tables store data indefinitely.

Question-39: Which statements are accurate about micro-partitions in Snowflake? (Select two.)

A. Their size is approximately 16MB.

B. They're compressed only if COMPRESS=TRUE is set on the table.

C. They are immutable.

D. They are encrypted exclusively in the Enterprise edition and above.

Correct Answer: A, C

Explanation: Micro-partitions in Snowflake are roughly 16MB in size and are immutable, meaning once written, they can't be changed. Compression isn't tied to a specific condition (COMPRESS=TRUE) and encryption isn't restricted to specific editions; all Snowflake data is encrypted.

Question-40: What techniques can Snowflake users employ to reduce data storage costs for short-lived tables? (Select two.)

A. Utilizing Temporary Tables

B. Using Transient Tables

C. Employing Provisional Tables

D. Leveraging Permanent Tables

Correct Answer: A, B

Explanation: Snowflake offers Temporary and Transient tables for managing short-lived data. Temporary tables are session-specific and get dropped at session end. Transient tables persist beyond the session but do not maintain historical data (Time Travel), lowering storage costs.

Question-41: What are the primary sections of the top navigation within the Snowflake User Interface (UI)? (Select three.)

A. Databases section

B. Tables section

C. Warehouses section

D. Worksheets section

Correct Answer: A, C, D

Explanation: The main sections in the top navigation of the Snowflake Web Interface are Databases, Warehouses, and Worksheets. Databases contain data, Warehouses provide computational resources for queries, and Worksheets enable executing SQL queries and scripts.

Question-42: Which data type is recommended for handling semi-structured data like JSON in Snowflake?

A. VARCHAR data type

B. RAW data type

C. LOB data type

D. VARIANT data type

Correct Answer: D

Explanation: For semi-structured data like JSON, Snowflake recommends using the VARIANT data type. VARIANT is versatile and self-describing, designed specifically to manage semi-structured data.

Question-43: Which statements are true regarding Snowflake network policies? A Snowflake network policy: (Select two.)

A. Is universally available across all Snowflake Editions

B. Is exclusively available to customers with Business Critical Edition

C. Can restrict or enable access to specific IP addresses

D. Can be activated through an 'ALTER DATABASE' command

Correct Answer: A, C

Explanation: Snowflake network policies are available across all Snowflake editions and can restrict or enable access to specific IP addresses, enhancing security.

Question-44: How long are query results stored in the Result Cache after their last access, assuming no data changes occur?

A. 1 Hour

B. 3 Hours

C. 12 hours

D. 24 hours

Correct Answer: D

Explanation: Query results remain in the Result Cache for 24 hours after their last access, provided no data changes occur.

This accelerates query performance if the same queries are rerun within this timeframe.

Question-45: Which connectors are available in the Downloads section of the Snowflake User Interface (UI)? (Select two.)

A. SnowSQL connector

B. ODBC connector

C. R connector

D. HIVE connector

Correct Answer: A, B

Explanation: The Downloads section of the Snowflake Web Interface provides access to SnowSQL and ODBC connectors. SnowSQL is a command-line client, while the ODBC connector is used by applications communicating with Snowflake through ODBC.

Question-46: Which of the following DML (Data Manipulation Language) commands is not supported by Snowflake?

A. UPSERT command

B. MERGE command

C. UPDATE command

D. TRUNCATE TABLE command

Correct Answer: A

Explanation: Snowflake does not support the UPSERT command. Instead, the MERGE command is provided, serving the same purpose as UPSERT.

Question-47: How long is the Query History retained in the Snowflake Web Interface (UI)?

A. About 60 minutes

B. Close to 24 hours

C. Approximately 14 days

D. Nearly 30 days

E. About 1 year

Correct Answer: C

Explanation: The Snowflake Web Interface retains Query History for approximately 14 days, aiding in audit, troubleshooting, or optimization activities.

Question-48: What's required to operate a Multi-Cluster Warehouse in auto-scale mode?

A. Adjust the Maximum Clusters setting to "Auto-Scale"

B. Set the Warehouse type to "Auto"

C. Ensure the Minimum Clusters and Maximum Clusters settings are the same

D. Set distinct values for Minimum Clusters and Maximum Clusters settings

Correct Answer: D

Explanation: Operating a Multi-Cluster Warehouse in auto-scale mode involves configuring different values for the Minimum Clusters and Maximum Clusters settings. This allows the system to adapt the cluster count based on load, balancing performance and cost.

Question-49: What choices are available when configuring a Virtual Warehouse? (Select two.)

A. Auto-drop

B. Auto-resize

C. Auto-resume

D. Auto-suspend

Correct Answer: C, D

Explanation: Virtual Warehouse setup options include Auto-resume and Auto-suspend. Auto-resume automatically restarts a suspended warehouse upon query submission, while Auto-suspend automatically suspends a warehouse after a period of inactivity.

Question-50: Which types of tables are excluded from the Fail-safe feature?

A. Temporary

B. Transient

C. Provisional

D. Permanent

Correct Answer: A, B

Explanation: The Fail-safe feature doesn't apply to Temporary and Transient table types in Snowflake. Fail-safe preserves data beyond the Time Travel retention period, safeguarding against accidental deletion or changes.

Question-51: What object among the following is not covered by Time Travel in Snowflake?

A. Tables

B. Schemas

C. Databases

D. Stages

Correct Answer: D

Explanation: Time Travel in Snowflake excludes Stages. While historical data from Tables, Schemas, and Databases within a specific time frame can be accessed using Time Travel, this feature does not apply to Stages.

Question-52: Which statement accurately describes the role of Micro-partition metadata in Snowflake?

A. This statement is completely accurate.

B. This statement is totally incorrect.

Correct Answer: A

Explanation: The statement is accurate. Micro-partition metadata in Snowflake enables certain operations to be performed without requiring Compute resources. This optimization enhances performance and reduces computational costs for tasks like row counting and data filtering.

Question-53: According to Snowflake's recommendations, which role(s) should at least be enrolled in Multi-Factor Authentication (MFA)?

A. SECURITYADMIN, ACCOUNTADMIN, PUBLIC, SYSADMIN

B. SECURITYADMIN, ACCOUNTADMIN, SYSADMIN

C. SECURITYADMIN, ACCOUNTADMIN

D. ACCOUNTADMIN

Correct Answer: D

Explanation: Snowflake advises that, at a minimum, all users assigned the ACCOUNTADMIN role should be registered for Multi-Factor Authentication (MFA). This additional layer of security helps ensure that users authenticate using multiple identification methods.

Question-54: Which two programming languages are suitable for crafting User Defined Functions (UDFs) in Snowflake?

A. Java

B. Javascript

C. SQL

D. Python

Correct Answer: B, C

Explanation: In Snowflake, User Defined Functions (UDFs) can be implemented using Javascript and SQL. This flexibility empowers developers to create intricate functions using familiar languages, enhancing their efficiency and effectiveness.

Question-55: Which statement accurately characterizes Multi-Factor Authentication (MFA) in Snowflake?

A. This statement is totally correct.

B. This statement is entirely incorrect.

Correct Answer: B

Explanation: The statement is incorrect. While Multi-Factor Authentication (MFA) in Snowflake can indeed be used in conjunction with Single Sign-On (SSO), it can also operate independently. Hence, the enhanced security of MFA is available even without employing SSO.

Question-56: Is the following assertion true? Snowflake cannot be accessed by third-party tools lacking a Snowflake-specific driver, but supporting standard JDBC or ODBC.

A. This statement is absolutely correct.

B. This statement is entirely wrong.

Correct Answer: A

Explanation: The statement is accurate. A third-party tool that exclusively supports standard JDBC or ODBC without a dedicated Snowflake driver would be unable to establish a connection with Snowflake. To ensure seamless integration with various applications and tools, Snowflake offers JDBC and ODBC drivers.

Question-57: Which statement precisely depicts the uniqueness and utility of Query ID's in Snowflake?

A. This statement is entirely accurate.

B. This statement is totally incorrect.

Correct Answer: A

Explanation: The statement is accurate. Query ID's in Snowflake are unique across all deployments and serve as identifiers that aid in troubleshooting and communication with Snowflake Support. These ID's facilitate pinpointing specific queries or issues for effective resolution.

Question-58: Which two factors play a pivotal role in determining the number of queries a Virtual Warehouse can concurrently handle in Snowflake?

A. The complexity of individual queries

B. The CONCURRENT_QUERY_LIMIT parameter set on the Snowflake account

C. The volume of data required for each query

D. The specific application or tool executing the query

Correct Answer: A, C

Explanation: The ability of a Virtual Warehouse to handle concurrent queries in Snowflake depends primarily on the intricacy of individual queries and the volume of data they involve. More complex or data-intensive queries necessitate more processing resources, potentially limiting the number of simultaneous queries.

Question-59: Regarding VALIDATION_MODE in Snowflake, which two statements accurately depict its behavior?

A. The VALIDATION_MODE option is used when establishing an Internal Stage

B. VALIDATION_MODE=RETURN_ALL_ERRORS is a parameter of the COPY command

C. The VALIDATION_MODE option verifies data integrity during the execution of the COPY statement, identifying rows that couldn't be loaded without errors

D. The VALIDATION_MODE option checks data accuracy during the COPY statement execution without completing the load, highlighting potential errors

Correct Answer: B, D

Explanation: In Snowflake, the VALIDATION_MODE option is integrated within the COPY command and primarily serves to validate data prior to loading. When set to RETURN_ALL_ERRORS, it enables comprehensive error identification during validation without loading the data, providing valuable insights into potential issues.

Question-60: Can some queries bypass the need for an active Virtual Warehouse by utilizing the metadata cache in Snowflake?

A. Always possible

B. Not at all possible

C. Only when the metadata cache is updated

D. Only with specific query types

Correct Answer: A

Explanation: Snowflake facilitates the execution of certain queries using the metadata cache, without requiring an active Virtual Warehouse. This feature optimizes query performance by eliminating the need to activate a Virtual Warehouse for specific scenarios, enhancing overall efficiency.

Question-61: Is it accurate that each worksheet within the Snowflake Web Interface (UI) can be associated with distinct roles, databases, schemas, and Virtual Warehouses?

A. Always possible

B. Not at all possible

C. Only when specific permissions are granted

D. Only with specific database schemas

Correct Answer: A

Explanation: Within the Snowflake Web Interface, every worksheet can be linked with various roles, databases, schemas, and Virtual Warehouses. This versatility empowers users to manage a diverse range of tasks and queries through a single interface, streamlining access control and permissions.

Question-62: At which level can the retention period for Time Travel be most precisely configured?

A. Account

B. Database

C. Schema

D. Table

Correct Answer: D

Explanation: The Time Travel feature in Snowflake allows the most precise configuration of the retention period at the level of a Table. This capability grants users the flexibility to access historical data from specific time periods, enhancing data recovery and analysis options.

Question-63: For which two types of workloads is Snowflake specifically designed?

A. OLAP (Analytics) workloads

B. OLTP (Transactional) workloads

C. Concurrent workloads

D. On-premise workloads

Correct Answer: A, C

Explanation: Snowflake's design primarily caters to OLAP (Online Analytical Processing) workloads and concurrent operations. It excels in supporting large-scale data warehousing, facilitating business analytics, and efficiently handling concurrent querying on extensive datasets.

Question-64: Which two statements accurately pertain to Snowpipe's functionality via the REST API?

A. It exclusively operates on Internal Stages

B. All COPY INTO options are available during Snowpipe's setup

C. Snowflake autonomously manages the computational resources required for executing COPY INTO commands in Snowpipe

D. Snowpipe effectively tracks the files it has ingested

Correct Answer: C, D

Explanation: Snowpipe via the REST API in Snowflake automatically manages the computational resources necessary for executing COPY INTO commands, ensuring smooth data ingestion. Additionally, it maintains a record of loaded files, preventing data duplication and conserving computational assets.

Question-65: Which two data formats are supported for unloading data from Snowflake?

A. Delimited formats such as CSV, TSV, etc.

B. Avro

C. JSON

D. ORC

Correct Answer: A, C

Explanation: Snowflake facilitates unloading data in delimited formats (CSV, TSV, etc.) and JSON. These formats are widely used for data exchange due to their simplicity, readability, and compatibility across different systems.

Question-66: Which of the following methods are valid for loading data into a Snowflake table?

A. Bulk copying from an External Stage

B. Continuous loading using Snowpipe REST API

C. Utilizing the Snowflake Web Interface (UI) data loading wizard

D. Bulk copying from an Internal Stage

Correct Answer: A, B, C

Explanation: Snowflake offers multiple avenues for data loading to accommodate diverse needs. These include bulk copying from an External Stage, continuous loading via the Snowpipe REST API, and utilizing the data loading wizard within the Snowflake Web Interface.

Question-67: Is it recommended practice to immediately assign a newly created custom role in Snowflake to the ACCOUNTADMIN role?

A. Always recommended

B. Never recommended

C. Recommended only for critical roles

D. Recommended only for non-critical roles

Correct Answer: B

Explanation: As a security best practice, it is generally not recommended to directly assign a freshly created custom role to the ACCOUNTADMIN role. This approach aligns with the principle of least privilege, ensuring roles are granted only essential privileges to mitigate unauthorized access risks.

Question-68: Is the statement true that a given table in Snowflake can solely be queried using the Virtual Warehouse employed for loading its data?

A. Absolutely Correct

B. Absolutely Incorrect

C. Might be Correct

D. Might be Incorrect

Correct Answer: B. Absolutely Incorrect

Explanation: The statement is incorrect. In Snowflake, a table is not restricted to being queried exclusively by the Virtual Warehouse used for loading its data. Snowflake's architecture, which includes shared data accessible by all compute resources, enables querying data across various Virtual Warehouses.

Question-69: Is it recommended practice to assign a clustering key to every table in Snowflake?

A. Absolutely Correct

B. Absolutely Incorrect

C. Might be Correct

D. Might be Incorrect

Correct Answer: B. Absolutely Incorrect

Explanation: While clustering keys can optimize storage and query performance, assigning them to every table is not a recommended practice. Clustering keys are most beneficial for larger tables and frequently queried tables with specific filtering requirements, and may not be suitable for every scenario.

Question-70: Can users execute queries using the query result cache in Snowflake without needing an active Warehouse?

A. Absolutely Possible

B. Absolutely Impossible

C. Might be Possible

D. Might be Impossible

Correct Answer: A. Absolutely Possible

Explanation: Snowflake enables querying the query result cache, even without an active Warehouse. If a query matches a previous query stored in the cache, Snowflake returns the cached results, optimizing performance and reducing the need for a running Warehouse.

Question-71: Which privileges are required to initiate the creation of a task within Snowflake?

A. The GLOBAL privilege CREATE TASK must be possessed by the user to start a new task.

B. The creation of tasks at the Application level necessitates the Account Admin role.

C. Most Snowflake DDLs operate as metadata operations exclusively; hence, executing CREATE TASK DDL does not require a virtual warehouse or task-specific grants.

D. Access to the target schema and the CREATE TASK privilege on the schema itself are mandatory for the role.

Correct Answer: D

Explanation: To create a task in Snowflake, the role must have both schema access and the CREATE TASK privilege on that schema. This ensures proper context and access control for task creation.

Question-72: How can one determine the required size of the virtual warehouse for a task?

A. Execute the root task concurrently to avoid overlooking execution instances.

B. Calculate warehouse size by querying the stream content's size, adjusting for larger content with larger warehouses.

C. Test-run a stored procedure executing individual SQL statements to initially gauge compute resource needs.

D. Set up the virtual warehouse with Multi-cluster warehouse (MCW) for automated concurrency aligned with task scheduling.

Correct Answer: C

Explanation: It is advisable to test-run the stored procedure with separate SQL statements to estimate the compute resource size needed for the task. This practice ensures the appropriate warehouse size for handling the task workload.

Question-73: Can Reader Accounts extract data from shared data objects for use external to Snowflake?

A. Absolutely Possible

B. Absolutely Impossible

C. Might be Possible

D. Might be Impossible

Correct Answer: A

Explanation: Reader accounts in Snowflake indeed have the capability to extract data from shared data objects for external use. This functionality enhances data sharing and flexibility.

Question-74: Is it feasible for users to visualize query result sets executed by other users sharing the same role?

A. Absolutely Possible

B. Absolutely Impossible

C. Might be Possible

D. Might be Impossible

Correct Answer: B

Explanation: In Snowflake, query results are not shared among users, even if they share the same role. Each user's query results remain isolated to maintain data security and privacy.

Question-75: In the Data Warehouse migration process to Snowflake, which element finds no place?

A. User Migration

B. Schema Migration

C. Index Migration

D. Data Pipeline Construction

Correct Answer: C

Explanation: Snowflake diverges from traditional indexing structures found in other databases. Thus, during the process of migrating to Snowflake, index migration is not applicable.

Question-76: If a role that owns two tables is created and subsequently dropped, who will become the new owner of those tables?

A. The tables will become orphaned.

B. The user who deleted the role will assume ownership.

C. SYSADMIN will take ownership.

D. The assumed role that dropped the initial role will become the owner.

Correct Answer: D

Explanation: When a role is dropped in Snowflake, the objects owned by that role shift ownership to the role active during the DROP ROLE command. Hence, the assumed role that initiated the role drop will become the owner of the two tables.

Question-77: Under what circumstances should auto-suspend be considered for deactivation in a Virtual Warehouse? Select two.

A. When users utilize compute resources at varying times within a 24/7 period.

B. When maintaining a consistent workload.

C. When immediate compute resource availability is crucial.

D. When avoiding manual Warehouse activation for user needs.

Correct Answer: B, C

Explanation: Disabling auto-suspend is suitable for sustaining a steady workload and for immediate compute resource availability. Auto-suspend can introduce small delays, which are undesirable for consistent workloads.

Question-78: Is the statement accurate that Snowflake bills a minimum of five minutes upon Virtual Warehouse activation?

A. The statement is completely correct.

B. The statement is partially correct.

C. The statement is completely incorrect.

D. The statement lacks sufficient context.

Correct Answer: C

Explanation: The statement is incorrect. Snowflake bills users per second of Virtual Warehouse usage, not subject to a minimum five-minute charge.

Question-79: Does federated authentication receive support from Snowflake across all editions?

A. Yes, it does support federated authentication in all editions.

B. No, it only supports federated authentication in select editions.

C. Yes, but only under specific circumstances.

D. No, it does not support federated authentication in any edition.

Correct Answer: A

Explanation: Snowflake indeed offers federated authentication in all editions, allowing users to employ their existing identity providers for authentication.

Question-80: Can Data Providers within Snowflake exclusively share data with the Data Consumer?

A. Yes, data sharing is restricted to the Data Consumer.

B. No, data can be shared beyond the Data Consumer.

C. Yes, but with specific prerequisites.

D. No, data sharing is entirely prohibited.

Correct Answer: B

Explanation: Data Providers in Snowflake can share data not only with Data Consumers but also with other Data Providers, facilitating broader information distribution.

Question-81: What services does Snowflake automatically manage for customers that might have been their responsibility in on-premise systems? Select all that apply.

A. Handling hardware installation and configuration

B. Executing software patching tasks

C. Ensuring physical security measures

D. Managing and maintaining metadata and statistics

Correct Answer: A, B, D

Explanation: Snowflake inherently handles hardware installation, software patching, and management of metadata and statistics. However, physical security is not managed by Snowflake as it's not relevant in a cloud environment.

Question-82: Is a Snowflake account billed for data stored in both Internal and External Stages?

A. Yes, billing occurs for both Internal and External Stages.

B. No, billing occurs only for the Internal Stages.

C. Yes, but only under specific circumstances.

D. No, there is no billing for either stage.

Correct Answer: B

Explanation: Snowflake bills for data storage in internal stages only. External stages (e.g., Amazon S3 or Google Cloud Storage) are billed directly by their respective cloud service providers, not by Snowflake.

Question-83: When a new Snowflake object is created, does it automatically become owned by the user who created it?

A. Yes, the user who creates the object becomes its owner.

B. No, ownership is not automatically assigned to the user who created the object.

C. Yes, but only under specific circumstances.

D. No, a different process governs ownership assignment.

Correct Answer: B

Explanation: In Snowflake, the role active during object creation becomes the owner, not the user who created the object.

Question-84: If a customer primarily uses SnowSQL / native connectors, does it preclude access to the Snowflake Web Interface (UI) without explicit support approval?

A. Yes, access to the UI requires explicit authorization.

B. No, using SnowSQL / native connectors does not impact UI access.

C. Yes, but under specific conditions.

D. No, UI access can only be granted by an administrator.

Correct Answer: B

Explanation: Using SnowSQL / native connectors does not restrict access to the Snowflake Web Interface. Users can access the UI without needing explicit support permission.

Question-85: What best characterizes Snowflake's database architecture?

A. It employs a columnar shared nothing architecture.

B. It operates on a shared disk architecture.

C. It utilizes a multi-cluster, shared data architecture.

D. It is built on a cloud-native shared memory architecture.

Correct Answer: C

Explanation: Snowflake employs a distinct multi-cluster, shared data architecture, enabling high scalability, performance, and concurrency.

Question-86: Is it possible to disable the fail-safe feature within a Snowflake account?

A. Yes, the fail-safe feature can be disabled.

B. No, the fail-safe feature cannot be disabled.

C. Yes, but only under specific circumstances.

D. No, fail-safe is a mandatory feature.

Correct Answer: B

Explanation: The fail-safe feature in Snowflake cannot be disabled. It is an inherent feature that provides a seven-day window for recovering accidentally modified or deleted data.

Question-87: How can the concept of 'clustering' be best described in Snowflake?

A. Clustering involves grouping and storing data within Snowflake's micro-partitions.

B. The database administrator defines the clustering approach for each Snowflake table.

C. The clustering key is a requisite for the COPY command when loading data into Snowflake.

D. Clustering can be deactivated within a Snowflake account.

Correct Answer: A

Explanation: Clustering in Snowflake refers to the organization of data within micro-partitions, optimizing query performance. The system, not the database administrator, automatically determines the clustering.

Question-88: Which command is used to set the Virtual Warehouse for a specific session?

A. Execute the command "COPY WAREHOUSE FROM <>"

B. Utilize the command "SET WAREHOUSE = <>"

C. Apply the command "USE WAREHOUSE <<warehouse name>>"

D. Implement the command "USE VIRTUAL_WAREHOUSE <>"

Correct Answer: C

Explanation: To designate the virtual warehouse for a session in Snowflake, utilize the "USE WAREHOUSE <<warehouse name>>" command. This command selects a warehouse for the current session, determining compute resources for subsequent queries and DDL statements.

Question-89: How can storage usage at the account level be monitored within Snowflake?

A. Access the Databases section on the Snowflake Web Interface (UI)

B. Navigate to Account -> Billing & Usage on the Snowflake Web Interface (UI)

C. Examine the Information Schema ->
ACCOUNT_USAGE_HISTORY View

D. Check the Account Usage Schema ->
ACCOUNT_USAGE_METRICS View

Correct Answer: B

Explanation: Monitor account-level storage usage by visiting
Account -> Billing & Usage in the Snowflake Web Interface
(UI). This section provides a comprehensive overview of
storage consumption.

Question-90: In Snowflake's architecture, where is metadata
statistics stored?

A. In the Storage Layer

B. Within the Compute Layer

C. Within the Database Layer

D. In the Cloud Services Layer

Correct Answer: D

Explanation: Metadata statistics are stored in Snowflake's
Cloud Services Layer. This layer manages metadata, query
optimization, access control, concurrency, and transactions.

Question-91: Which of these connectors support Multi-
Factor Authentication (MFA) authorization during
connection? (Choose all that apply.)

A. JDBC

B. SnowSQL

C. Snowflake Web Interface (UI)

D. ODBC

E. Python

Correct Answer: A, B, C, D, E

Explanation: All listed connectors - JDBC, SnowSQL, Snowflake Web Interface (UI), ODBC, and Python - support Multi-Factor Authentication (MFA) authorization when connecting to Snowflake, enhancing security.

Question-92: Statement: Only External Stages can be referenced as a source via Snowpipe using the REST API.

A. Always applicable

B. Sometimes applicable

C. Rarely applicable

D. Never applicable

Correct Answer: D

Explanation: The statement is false. Snowpipe, through the REST API, can reference both external stages and named internal stages as sources, offering data loading flexibility.

Question-93: Statement: Creating a named File Format object is a prerequisite for loading data into Snowflake.

A. This is a compulsory requirement

B. It's an optional requirement

C. This is rarely needed

D. It's never a requirement

Correct Answer: A

Explanation: This statement is true. While data can be loaded into Snowflake without a named File Format object, creating one often enhances loading efficiency.

Question-94: What is the maximum compressed row size allowed in Snowflake?

A. 8KB

B. 16MB

C. 50MB

D. 4000GB

Correct Answer: B

Explanation: Snowflake permits a maximum compressed row size of 16MB. Any rows exceeding this size during loading result in an error.

Question-95: Statement: AWS Private Link establishes a secure connection from an on-premise data center to Snowflake.

A. Always True

B. Sometimes True

C. Rarely True

D. Never True

Correct Answer: D

Explanation: The statement is incorrect. AWS Private Link establishes a secure connection between AWS VPCs and Snowflake, not from an on-premise data center.

Question-96: Statement: Compression during data unloading in Snowflake is exclusively applicable to JSON and CSV files.

A. Always applicable

B. Sometimes applicable

C. Rarely applicable

D. Never applicable

Correct Answer: D

Explanation: This statement is false. Although Snowflake supports unloading data in CSV and JSON formats, it doesn't restrict compression to these file types.

Question-97: Statement: Provisioning a 4X-Large Warehouse in Snowflake can occasionally take longer than an X-Small Warehouse.

A. Always True

B. Sometimes True

C. Rarely True

D. Never True

Correct Answer: A

Explanation: The statement is true. Depending on demand, provisioning a larger warehouse, like a 4X-Large Warehouse, might take more time than provisioning a smaller one.

Question-98: The Information Schema and Account Usage Share provide storage information. Identify the three objects for which these resources offer information.

A. User information

B. Table structures and their associated data

C. Database details

D. Information about Internal Stages

Correct Answer: B, C, D

Explanation: The Information Schema and Account Usage Share offer crucial insights into the storage status of tables, databases, and internal stages within a data management system. They do not provide direct information about users.

Question-99: Is the statement "The source data files for loading into Snowflake must not exceed 16MB in size" true or false?

A. The statement is true, and the maximum allowable file size is indeed 16MB.

B. The statement is not correct; there is no such file size limitation.

C. The statement is partly correct, but the file size limit is different.

D. The statement is completely misleading; there is no restriction on file sizes.

Correct Answer: B

Explanation: Snowflake does not impose a maximum file size limit for loading data. While breaking data into smaller parts can optimize loading, there is no strict 16MB size restriction.

Question-100: Assess the accuracy of this statement: "Reader Accounts do not result in additional Compute costs for the Data Provider, as they only access shared data without making any changes."

A. The statement accurately represents the cost structure.

B. The statement is incorrect, as additional Compute costs can be incurred.

C. The statement might hold true in specific circumstances, but not universally.

D. The statement is misleading as it depends on the data provider's policies and agreements.

Correct Answer: B

Explanation: While Reader Accounts primarily access shared data for reading, they do generate additional compute costs. These costs arise from executing queries against the shared data. Despite not altering the data, the computational resources used for query processing translate to costs.

www.ingramcontent.com/pod-product-compliance
Lightning Source LLC
La Vergne TN
LVHW051654050326
832903LV00032B/3801